P9-AEU-673

Microwave Cook Book

By the Editors of Sunset Books and Sunset Magazine

Lane Publishing Co. • **Menlo Park, California**

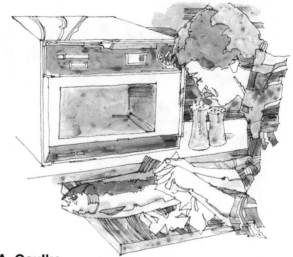

Edited by Judith A. Gaulke

Research and Text: Cynthia Scheer

Assistant Editors: Joan Griffiths, Linda Selden
Design: Cynthia Hanson
Illustrations: Dick Cole

Cover: Chicken Teriyaki with Vegetables (see page 45).
    Photograph by Darrow M. Watt.

Editor, Sunset Books: David E. Clark

Sixth Printing January 1979

World rights reserved. Copyright © Lane Publishing Co.,
Menlo Park, CA 94025. No part of this publication may be
reproduced by any mechanical, photographic, or electronic
process or in the form of a phonographic recording, nor may
it be stored in a retrieval system, transmitted, or otherwise
copied for public or private use without prior written
permission from the publisher. Library of Congress No.
75-26491. ISBN Title No. 0-376-02502-6. Lithographed in
the United States.

Contents

Special Features

Microwave Magic

The "today" way of cooking...cool, clean, speedy

Why Cook with Microwaves?

Microwave cookery can liberate the cook. It is speedy, cool, clean cooking that gets you in and out of the kitchen in no time.

That's not to say short cooking times inhibit a relaxed, creative approach to cooking; and don't think you have to forget what you already know about cooking. You control how you cook.

Opening the microwave oven door shuts off the unit so you can stir, turn, and check for doneness with ease—without facing that blast of hot air you get from your conventional oven.

Through the closed door, you can watch all the action, hear the food sizzling away, and sniff familiar aromas.

Microwave cooking saves time over regular cooking—in some instances, a great deal of time. (But in some other cases, such as with long grain rice and pasta, cooking times are about the same.) So what you've heard is true—a bacon slice cooks crisp in a minute, a potato in about four.

The beauty of the oven is its ability to thaw food fast, shorten cooking time, and reheat leftovers quickly without drying them out—a boon to families with erratic eating schedules. Because you can cook and serve in the same container, after-dinner clean-up is a breeze. And spatters can be quickly wiped off the cool oven walls. To top it all, with quick-cooking dishes, microwave cooking can also be a saver of energy—yours and the household's too.

How Does It Work?

To understand what the oven can do, you need to know a little about how it works. The mechanics are simple. Inside the microwave oven is a magnetron vacuum tube. It converts ordinary household electrical energy into high frequency microwaves.

These waves are either reflected, passed through, or absorbed by different materials. Metals reflect them (the oven walls are generally metal); glass, pottery, paper, and most plastics allow them to pass through (cooking utensils must be nonmetallic); and foods absorb them.

A stirrer fan, located in the top of most ovens, circulates the microwaves around the oven for more even energy distribution.

How Do Microwaves Cook Food?

Microwaves are absorbed by the moisture in food. The absorbed microwave energy causes the food molecules to vibrate rapidly, producing heat to cook the food. Since the waves penetrate deeply into the food, the interior begins to cook as well as the exterior. This accounts for the speed of microwave cooking.

In a conventional oven, heat is applied only to the outside surface of the food; it penetrates by conduction. Since foods are generally poor conductors, the outside may be cooked before the center is evenly heated.

The air in the microwave oven is not affected by microwaves and stays cool. Yet cooking containers may pick up some heat from the food itself, so you will need to keep pot holders on hand when a recipe calls for longer cooking.

What Affects Cooking Time?

Timing is the magic word. Because microwave ovens vary from one manufacturer to the other, cooking times can vary.

Our recipe times may be different from those called for in the manual that came with your microwave oven. Use our cooking times as approximate guides and then check for doneness as suggested in each recipe.

Here are some points that affect timing in microwave cooking:

• The quantity of food in the oven. More food means more time. While a single potato cooks in four minutes, two potatoes may take up to twice as long. Never vary the quantities in these recipes without considering that timing will change.

• The temperature of the food. More time is needed to cook cold foods, as more energy must be absorbed to heat them.

• Dense foods take longer than light, fluffy mixtures since the waves penetrate less easily.

• Foods with a great deal of moisture cook faster than drier foods or those that are not as fresh.

• Arrangement of food in the oven. Distribute food evenly. Our recipes suggest turning containers and rearranging food during cooking to compensate for any unevenness.

• Because food continues to cook after you remove it from the oven, you must allow for a "standing time." This is particularly important with thick, dense foods, such as roasts. More about this when we discuss how we tested our recipes.

How Do Ovens Differ?

Today's microwave ovens are much more sophisticated than those that first came on the market. Now you can choose style and size as well as a number of cooking features.

The countertop portable model is still the most popular oven. It can be moved from place to place (kitchen to patio, old home to new), takes up little room, is easy to clean, and can be installed in a wall, if you wish. Two models are available—one model operating on 600–650 watts, and another smaller, less expensive model operating on 450–500 watts. All our recipes were tested in 600–650-watt models. Owners of the smaller models should extend cooking times for our recipes.

No special installation procedures are required for portable models, except for the important proviso that they must be plugged into grounded 115 or 120-volt electrical outlets.

Double ovens can be free-standing or built in. The microwave oven is usually on top, the conventional one on the bottom.

Combination ovens are available, too. This means microwave and conventional cooking can be done in the same oven using the two cooking methods simultaneously or independently.

What About Different Oven Power Settings?

Since we'd like all microwave oven owners to be able to use this cook book, we have included very few recipes that use anything but the regular full power setting available on all ovens, old or new.

Newer ovens have an increasing number of options besides the regular full power setting—defrost, low power, variable power, browning elements, and turntables. (Another option offered by some manufacturers is a special timing knob for use by those who are blind.)

Automatic defrosting and low power settings offer basically the same advantages. Here's how they work: the oven shuts itself off and on. This means microwaves are transmitted, then interrupted for a specific time period (usually about 30 seconds) for the food to "rest." This "rest" period allows energy to be transferred from the food surface it first enters into other parts of the food. The result is more even cooking or defrosting without collecting energy all in one area. Frozen food no longer starts to cook around the fringes while staying icy inside as it would if the oven were just turned on to the regular full power setting.

You can defrost food manually in models having only the regular full power setting; do this by turning the oven on and off for specific lengths of time. This creates a "resting" period, just as the automatic setting would. For all defrosting timetables, consult your microwave manual.

A variable power setting is another feature offered on some machines. This setting automatically turns the magnetron tube on and off at split-second intervals within the cooking time.

A browning element, a built-in feature of some ovens, can be turned on when the microwave energy is off. It is not designed for cooking, only browning. (You can place the food under your conventional broiler for the same effect.)

A turntable is a feature at least one manufacturer makes available. It's a tray in the bottom of the oven that rotates the dish of food, exposing all sides to microwaves.

What Utensils to Use

Your choice of cooking containers for the microwave oven depends on one thing— whether or not the microwaves can pass through the container to reach the food. There are many utensils to choose from: glass, pottery, china (without gold or silver trim), woven baskets, paper, and some plastics. Check your manufacturer's manual for specifics. Avoid using wooden containers; you run the risk of cracking them.

Many foods can be heated directly in their serving dishes—soup in bowls or a tureen, coffee in cups, a whole meal on a dinner plate. Whenever possible, consider using a container you can carry right to the table to save yourself cleanup time.

Remember, do not use any metal container or porcelain-coated metal container. The metal will reflect the microwaves away from the food. The food can't absorb the microwaves, and it won't cook. You also run the risk of reflecting the microwaves back at the magnetron tube, damaging or even ruining it.

Thermometers made especially for microwave ovens are available but can be used in an oven only when specified by that oven's manufacturer. Check your microwave manual.

To take the temperature reading with a standard meat thermometer, remove food from the oven and insert the thermometer into the thickest portion; let stand about 10 minutes to register the internal temperature. If more cooking is needed, remove the thermometer and return the food to the oven. Some newer ovens have an automatic cooking control—temperature sensing probe—that can be inserted into a roast or other food while in the oven. When the food reaches a preset temperature, the oven shuts off automatically.

Nonmetallic racks, available through microwave oven dealers, elevate foods (such as chicken) above their own juices when cooking. The racks come with or without their own cooking dish. Often an inverted saucer or small plate in a baking dish can do the same job.

Browning utensils (trays, grills, and dishes) are also available through microwave dealers. They duplicate the conventional searing of frying-pan cooking. You preheat the browning utensil in the microwave oven and then place the food to be cooked on the heated surface. Actually, only the very outer surface of the food becomes hot. If you turn the food over, the browning utensil will have lost much of its heat to the first side cooked. To sear the other side, you may need to remove the food and reheat the utensil.

How We Tested Our Recipes

To minimize cleanup, we tried in most of our testing to confine cooking to just one container for each recipe. Our favorite all-purpose cooking container was a shallow glass or ceramic 7 by 11-inch baking dish (2-qt. size). It fits into all microwave ovens and food can be spread out for more even cooking. You will see it called for in many of our recipes. (It's preferable to a deep 2-quart baking dish, in which the food forms a thicker layer.)

No aluminum foil wrap was used in our testing, but some oven manufacturers say small pieces can be used to protect areas you don't want overcooked, such as ends of chicken legs. Check your manufacturer's manual.

Clear plastic film was used to cover all cooking containers in our recipes unless stated otherwise. Plastic film holds moisture in tightly, and we wanted that. If the food is to be covered loosely, it is indicated in the recipe. Other covers that can be used are glass lids, paper towels, paper napkins, wax paper, and plates.

Remember to lift any cover carefully away from you to allow steam to escape before you reach in to stir or test for doneness.

For fasteners, such as are needed to tie chicken legs together, we used string, twine, or wooden picks. Do not use metal twists—even that small amount of metal would interfere with microwaves.

Every microwave oven produces a slightly irregular pattern of waves. That means food cooks faster in some parts of the oven. To compensate, you should arrange the food as evenly as possible at the beginning and then turn, stir, or rearrange it during cooking as our recipes suggest. This uneven pattern is not a manufacturing defect. It is caused by resonance and can be compared to the acoustics of a concert hall.

A "standing time" is called for in many recipes. Foods continue to cook after they're taken out of the oven. Since heat is still being conducted from the outside to the center of the food, this period allows for evening-up of heat and a finishing-off of the cooking process.

What About Oven Safety?

Microwave ovens are as safe as any other kitchen heating appliance. Microwaves are nonionizing radiant energy, the same as radio waves. Very different, though, from ionizing X-rays, microwaves do not cause any chemical change. No harmful radiation is produced.

Ovens are strictly designed to contain the energy produced by the microwaves inside. Safety door seals and automatic shut-off switches prevent any generating of microwave energy when the door is open. The user is never exposed to microwaves.

Individuals wearing pacemakers should always be aware when entering a kitchen or restaurant where a microwave oven might be in operation. Pacemaker manufacturers give the wearer warning of this and other environments that might interrupt transmission—car motors, electric razors, and elevators.

Microwave oven manufacturers follow stringent safety standards set by the United States Government under the Federal Safety Performance Standards for Microwave Ovens, Department of Health, Education, and Welfare rules.

Appetizers

Hot hors d'oeuvres:
guests marvel while you mingle

When you're entertaining, your performing microwave oven quickly steals center stage. But you, the host or hostess, get all the credit for so quickly serving those piping hot hors d'oeuvres.

Many appetizers can be made on the spot and served. Others can be prepared ahead, refrigerated, and popped into the oven for almost instant serving when needed. Heat appetizers right on their serving plates for added convenience; then mingle with your guests and enjoy the party.

Develop a working knowledge of which appetizers can be cooked successfully in a microwave oven. Many of your favorite tidbits adapt well to electronic cooking—others do not. For example, any appetizers encased in a crust or batter are poor candidates, even if baked or deep-fried beforehand; the coating becomes soggy.

Yet cheesy snacks—dips, spreads, fondues—do very well. They melt rapidly and can be reheated immediately to new life when they've cooled. Use cheeses such as jack, fontina, teleme, Swiss, Longhorn Cheddar, and process cheeses.

Cooking a large quantity of an appetizer in the microwave oven can take more time than in a conventional oven. So if you're cooking for a crowd, it may make sense to prepare a large number of hors d'oeuvres all at once in your regular oven or under the broiler, then serve; or simply rely on the microwave oven to reheat them. Bacon-wrapped tidbits are a good example—you can broil a large number at once in less time than it takes to cook half a dozen or so electronically.

This chapter starts you out with easily prepared cheese appetizers, followed by more elaborate meatball, seafood, and vegetable treats.

Appetizer Parmesan Fondue

You can serve a sizable group of friends with this reheatable, garlicky fondue. Cook it in a ceramic pot; then place pot over a candle warmer or in simmering water to keep fondue warm. Dip it up with cubes of French bread.

2 large packages (8 oz. *each*) cream cheese or Neufchatel
About 2 cups milk
2 small cloves garlic, pressed (or 1 teaspoon garlic salt)
1 package (5 oz.) Parmesan cheese, shredded or grated (about 1½ cups)
Salt to taste
Freshly ground pepper and thinly sliced green onion
1 loaf (about 1 pound) sourdough French bread, cut in 1-inch cubes

Put cream cheese into a ceramic serving container (about 1½-quart size). Cook, uncovered, in the microwave oven 2 minutes to soften. Gradually stir in milk until blended into a smooth sauce. Add garlic and Parmesan cheese. Cook, uncovered, 3 to 4 minutes, stirring once or twice until cheese melts and thickens. Add salt to taste and more milk if needed for good dipping consistency.

Serve sprinkled with freshly ground pepper and green onions. Reheat fondue briefly in the microwave oven if it cools. Offer French bread cubes and fondue forks or long wooden skewers for dipping. Makes about 1 quart fondue. Serves 12 to 16 as an appetizer.

Jack Quesadillas

In just 30 seconds, you can be eating a folded flour tortilla treat with cheese inside. Heat quesadillas one at a time; then cut in wedges and serve.

Shredded jack cheese
Flour tortilla
Mexican seasoning or crushed red pepper
Soft butter or margarine
Grated Parmesan cheese

For each quesadilla, scatter about 2 tablespoons jack cheese on half of a flour tortilla, not quite to the edge. Sprinkle lightly with Mexican seasoning. Fold tortilla in half; press gently together. Lightly spread top with butter; then sprinkle lightly with grated Parmesan cheese. Place on a plate in the microwave oven and cook, uncovered, 30 seconds or until cheese melts. Cut in wedges and serve. Makes 3 or 4 appetizers.

Green Chile and Cheese Dip

Choose a ceramic or pottery serving dish in which to cook this colorful, mildly hot chile dip.

2 tablespoons salad oil
2 medium-size onions, chopped
1 tablespoon all-purpose flour
½ cup regular-strength chicken broth
½ cup sour cream
1 can (4 oz.) California green chiles, seeded and chopped
1 can (4 oz.) pimientos, drained and chopped
3 cups shredded mild Cheddar or Longhorn cheese
Tortilla chips

Pour salad oil in a 1-quart dish you can later serve the dip from; heat in the microwave oven for 1 minute. Add onions and cook, uncovered, 4 minutes or until soft; stir often. Blend in flour and gradually add chicken broth. Stir in sour cream. Heat, uncovered, 1 minute until slightly thickened. Add chiles and pimientos to sauce; then gradually stir in cheese until melted. (If necessary, heat mixture in oven 1 to 2 minutes to completely melt cheese.)

Place over a candle warmer or on an electric warming tray. Serve with tortilla chips. Makes 2½ cups or about 12 appetizer servings.

Burrito Tidbits

Need a quick appetizer when you're entertaining many people? Just roll flour tortillas around a spicy sausage-cheese filling, heat, and slice into bite-size burritos.

1 package (12 to 14 oz.) chorizo sausages
1 dozen flour tortillas
3 cups shredded jack cheese

Remove casings from sausages; crumble meat into 1½-quart baking dish. Cook, uncovered, in the microwave oven 3 minutes, stirring 2 or 3 times, until meat is firm and looks darker in color. Drain and discard drippings. Sprinkle about 2 tablespoons meat down the center of each tortilla. Sprinkle meat in each tortilla with about ¼ cup cheese. Roll up tortilla snugly; place, seam side down, on a paper plate or serving dish. Heat 3 rolls at a time, uncovered, for about 1½ minutes or until cheese is melted. Cut each roll into 4 slices and serve warm. Makes 48 appetizers.

Mexican Bean Dip

For an at-home fiesta or for spur-of-the-moment entertaining, turn to this easy dip with an authentic Mexican touch.

  1 **can (1 lb.) refried beans**
  1 **cup shredded Cheddar cheese**
  ½ **cup thinly sliced green onions**
  ¼ **teaspoon salt**
    Dash *each* **ground cumin and coriander**
  2 **tablespoons taco sauce or green chile salsa**
    Tortilla chips or corn chips

In a 1-quart serving dish or pottery casserole, mix together the beans, cheese, onions, salt, cumin, coriander, and taco sauce. Cook, covered, in the microwave oven 4 to 5 minutes, stirring several times, until mixture is hot and bubbly and cheese is melted. Serve with tortilla chips or corn chips. Makes about 2½ cups (about 12 appetizer servings).

Mushrooms with Herbs

Instant minced onion is a seasoning short-cut here. Serve the mushrooms in a chafing dish.

  1½ **pounds mushrooms,** *each* **about 1-inch size (about 7 dozen mushrooms)**
  2 **tablespoons butter or margarine**
  1 **tablespoon instant minced onion**
  1 **teaspoon** *each* **dry basil and oregano leaves**
  ¼ **teaspoon** *each* **thyme leaves, garlic salt, and liquid hot pepper seasoning**
  1 **tablespoon lime juice**
  2 **tablespoons dry Sherry**

Twist out mushroom stems (save for other uses). Wash mushroom caps; pat dry. In a 7 by 11-inch baking dish, melt butter 1 minute in the microwave oven. To the butter add onion, basil, oregano, thyme, garlic salt, hot pepper seasoning, lime juice, and Sherry, mixing well. Add mushrooms and coat with mixture.

Cook, uncovered, 5 to 6 minutes, stirring often. Serve in a chafing dish or over a candle warmer. Makes about 7 dozen appetizers.

Hot Mushroom Canapés

Rich brown cream coats thin mushroom slices to make an impressive hors d'oeuvre that requires very little effort. Offer it from a chafing dish; serve over toasted bread rounds or Melba toast.

  2 **cups sliced large mushrooms (about 10 mushrooms,** *each* **1½ inches in diameter)**
    Salt
  1 **cup whipping cream**
    Small toasted bread rounds or Melba toast

Place mushrooms in a 7 by 11-inch baking dish. Sprinkle lightly with salt and cover with whipping cream. Cook, uncovered, in the microwave oven 12 to 14 minutes, stirring occasionally, until cream is very thick and browned.

Transfer to a chafing dish and keep hot. To serve, spoon onto each toast round a slice or two of mushroom well covered with brown cream. Makes 3 to 4 dozen appetizers.

Bubbly Cheese and Crackers

Here's an easy twist to an old standby. Instead of plain old cheese and cracker snacks, melt cheese right on the crackers in seconds in the microwave oven. These cheeses melt smoothly—jack, fontina, Swiss, Longhorn Cheddar, and process cheese.

You'll need a sturdy cracker that won't go limp from the moisture released as the cheese melts. Good choices are shredded wheat or thin wheat crackers, Melba toast, and crisp rye crackers.

Make a few appetizers at a time by placing 6 crackers on a serving plate (more will take more cooking time). Top each with a ¾-inch cube of cheese. Heat, uncovered, in the microwave oven 30 to 45 seconds or until cheese is melted and bubbly (turn plate, if necessary, to cook cheese evenly). Makes 6 appetizers at a time.

Quick Cheese Dip

Scooped onto tortilla chips and accompanied by taco sauce, melted jack cheese makes a nothing-to-it treat to serve last-minute guests.

  1 **pound jack cheese, sliced ¼ inch thick**
    Tortilla chips
    Taco sauce or green chile salsa

(Continued on next page)

Arrange about half the cheese in a single layer in a baking dish or ceramic serving dish. Heat, uncovered, in the microwave oven 1½ minutes, turning dish and stirring 2 or 3 times. Cheese should be soft and bubbly throughout. Keep it warm over a candle warmer or on an electric warming tray. Scoop up with tortilla chips, spooning a little taco sauce over tops. Melt remaining cheese as you need it. Makes 8 to 10 servings.

Almond Shrimp

For a hearty, aromatic appetizer, present these big, garlic-flavored shrimp in a chafing dish or on an electric warming tray.

  ½ **cup (¼ lb.) butter or margarine**
  3 **cloves garlic, minced or pressed**
  ½ **cup sliced almonds**
  2 **pounds medium-size shrimp, shelled and deveined**
  ½ **cup chopped parsley**
    Lemon wedges

Melt butter in a 7 by 11-inch baking dish for 45 seconds in the microwave oven. Add garlic and almonds; cook, uncovered, 1 minute, stirring once or twice. Add shrimp and cook, uncovered, 5 minutes or until shrimp are bright pink; stir once. Blend in parsley. Transfer to a warming tray or place in a chafing dish to serve with wooden picks. Accompany with lemon wedges. Makes about 5 dozen appetizers.

Chinese Stuffed Mushrooms

Fill large mushroom caps with ground pork, shrimp, and water chestnuts for a savory morsel with crunch. In the microwave oven, the mushrooms steam in their own moisture.

 16 **to 18 mushrooms, about 1½ inches in diameter**
  6 **ounces raw shrimp, shelled and deveined**
  5 **canned water chestnuts, drained**
  ½ **pound lean ground pork**
  1 **clove garlic, minced or pressed**
  ⅛ **teaspoon ground ginger (optional)**
  2 **tablespoons cornstarch**
  ½ **teaspoon sugar**
  2 **tablespoons soy sauce**
 16 **to 18 small sprigs fresh coriander (Chinese parsley or cilantro) or ¼ to ½ teaspoon dry cilantro leaves, crushed**

Wash and dry mushrooms carefully. Twist out stems to make hollow cups (save stems for other uses). Finely chop shrimp and water chestnuts. Mix together with ground pork until blended; add garlic. Lightly mix in ginger (if used), cornstarch, sugar, and soy sauce. Divide meat mixture evenly among mushrooms, mounding into each cavity. Top each with a sprig of coriander or a light sprinkling of dry cilantro leaves. Arrange filled mushrooms in a 7 by 11-inch baking dish; cover and cook in the microwave oven 8 to 10 minutes or until meat mixture is firm. Turn dish 3 or 4 times during cooking. Makes 16 to 18 appetizers.

Artichoke Nibbles

Bake this zesty mixture of chopped marinated artichokes and Cheddar cheese in just 10 minutes; then cut it in squares. It's tasty served hot or at room temperature.

  2 **jars (6 oz. *each*) marinated artichoke hearts**
  1 **small onion, finely chopped**
  1 **clove garlic, minced or pressed**
  4 **eggs**
  ¼ **cup fine dry bread crumbs**
  ¼ **teaspoon salt**
  ⅛ **teaspoon *each* pepper, oregano leaves, and liquid hot pepper seasoning**
  ½ **pound sharp Cheddar cheese, shredded (about 2 cups)**
  2 **tablespoons minced parsley**

Drain marinade from 1 jar artichokes into a 7 by 11-inch baking dish. Drain other jar (you might save marinade for other uses). Chop all artichokes; set aside. Add onion and garlic to dish and cook, uncovered, 4 minutes in the microwave oven until onion is limp, stirring once or twice.

    In a bowl, beat eggs slightly with a fork. Add crumbs, salt, pepper, oregano, and hot pepper seasoning. Stir in cheese, parsley, and artichokes; pour mixture into baking dish with onions. Cook, uncovered, 10 to 12 minutes or until set in center when lightly touched. Turn dish several times. Let cool in dish 10 minutes; cut into 1-inch squares. Serve warm or at room temperature. Makes about 6 dozen appetizers.

Savory Artichokes

A delicate cheese dollop puffs up in the middle of each artichoke bottom in this elegant, easy-to-eat appetizer.

1 package (3 oz.) cream cheese, at room
 temperature
2 tablespoons fresh or freeze-dried chopped
 chives
2 tablespoons softened butter
1 jar (16 oz.) artichoke bottoms (crowns),
 drained
 Salt and pepper
¼ cup grated Parmesan cheese
 Paprika

Beat together cream cheese, chives, and butter.
Arrange artichokes, hollow side up, in a circle
on a large glass or ceramic plate. Sprinkle lightly
with salt and pepper. Top each with a rounded
teaspoon of cheese mixture. Sprinkle evenly with
Parmesan cheese. Cook, uncovered, in microwave oven 3 minutes, turning plate 2 times, until
cheese is bubbling and puffy. Sprinkle lightly with
paprika. Makes 15 to 18 appetizers.

Pâté with Sherry

A blender and a microwave oven work hand in
hand to cut preparation time down to virtually
nothing for this Sherry-flavored pâté. The recipe
is based on 1 pound of chicken livers—buy them
by the pound or accumulate them in your freezer
from the chickens you use. Pâté is best if made
a day ahead so flavors have a chance to blend.
You can keep it refrigerated up to 5 days or
freeze it for later use.

¾ cup (⅜ lb.) butter or margarine
1 pound chicken livers, chopped
2 cloves garlic, minced or pressed
1¼ teaspoons Worcestershire
½ teaspoon salt
¼ teaspoon pepper
⅓ cup dry Sherry
1 hard-cooked egg, chopped (optional)
 Thinly sliced green onion or toasted
 slivered almonds
 Crisp crackers or Melba toast

In a 9-inch-square baking dish, melt butter in the
microwave oven 2 minutes. Add chicken livers
and garlic and cook, covered, 3 to 4 minutes or
until liver loses pinkness; stir several times. Add
Worcestershire, salt, pepper, and Sherry. Place
in blender container and whirl until smooth.
Lightly mix in hard-cooked egg, if used. Spoon
into serving dish; cover and chill at least 1 day
to blend flavors. Garnish with onion or almonds;
serve with crackers. Makes about 2½ cups.
Serves 12 to 16 as an appetizer.

Glazed Sausage Balls

A fragrant sauce with surprising ingredients—
coriander, allspice, apple jelly, and chutney—
glazes these hefty appetizer meatballs.

⅓ pound bulk pork sausage
¾ pound lean ground beef
½ teaspoon *each* salt, dry mustard, and
 coriander seed (crushed)
¼ teaspoon ground allspice
1 egg
¼ cup *each* fine dry bread crumbs and
 thinly sliced green onions
½ cup *each* apple jelly and Major Grey's
 chutney (finely chopped)
1 teaspoon lemon juice

In a large bowl, combine sausage, ground beef,
salt, dry mustard, coriander seed, allspice, egg,
bread crumbs, and onions. Shape into 1-inch
balls (refrigerate or freeze if made ahead). Arrange meatballs (thawed if frozen) in single layer
in shallow baking dish. Cook, covered, in the microwave oven 5 minutes, turning dish and stirring
meatballs once; drain and discard drippings.

In a glass measuring cup, combine apple jelly,
chutney, and lemon juice. Cook, uncovered, 1½
minutes or until mixture is bubbly around edges
and jelly is melted. Pour over meatballs. Stir to
coat all surfaces well. Transfer to a chafing dish
and keep warm. Makes about 48 appetizers.

Bagna Cauda Dipping Sauce

Crisp, fresh vegetables are inviting when served
alongside garlicky butter sauce for dipping.
Choose 3 or 4 of your favorite ones to serve raw.
Try small zucchini (sliced lengthwise), cauli-
flowerettes, or crunchy turnip or jicama slices.

½ cup (¼ lb.) butter or margarine
¼ cup olive oil
4 small cloves garlic, pressed
1 can (2 oz.) flat anchovy fillets, well drained
 Assorted fresh raw vegetables

In serving bowl, combine butter, olive oil, and
garlic. Finely chop anchovy fillets and add to
sauce. Cook, uncovered, in the microwave oven
1 minute or until butter melts. Stir well. Set over
a candle or low alcohol flame. Mixture must not
get hot enough to brown and burn. Serve with
raw vegetables to dip. Serves 10 as an appetizer.

Roasted and Flavored Nuts and Seeds

For between-meal snacks or appetizer nibbles when entertaining, try toasting a variety of nuts and seeds to a golden hue in the microwave oven to bring out their rich, full flavor.

Chestnuts can be ready to peel and enjoy in less than 5 minutes (they take 40 minutes or more in a regular oven). And, depending on time of year, you can roast your own pumpkin seeds, sunflower seeds, and such winter squash seeds as Danish or butternut.

If nuts are prepared ahead, cool them completely and store airtight until needed.

Chestnuts. The nut shell must be slashed before roasting to prevent chestnuts from exploding when heated. Make crisscross cuts piercing the shells of 1½ to 2 dozen chestnuts. Place nuts in a single layer in a shallow dish; cook, uncovered, in the microwave oven 1 minute. Turn nuts over; cook 1 minute. Stir well and cook 1 minute more or until nuts are soft when squeezed. Remove from oven and let stand 5 minutes or until cool enough to peel off shell. Nuts are best eaten while still warm (or reheat in microwave oven for 30 seconds).

Roasted Almonds and Pine Nuts. Spread ½ cup blanched whole or slivered almonds (or pine nuts) in a single layer in a shallow dish. Cook, uncovered, in the microwave oven 6 to 8 minutes or until golden. Stir once every few minutes.

Curried Almonds. Stir together 1 teaspoon curry powder, ½ teaspoon seasoned salt, and ⅛ teaspoon garlic powder; set aside.

Roast 1 cup whole blanched or unblanched almonds in the microwave oven according to previous directions. When nuts are golden, drizzle 2 teaspoons salad oil evenly over top, sprinkle with curry mixture, and stir well. Cook, uncovered, 2 to 3 minutes, stirring often to blend flavors well.

Garlic Almonds. Stir together ½ teaspoon garlic salt and ¼ teaspoon *each* garlic powder and paprika; set aside.

Roast 1 cup whole blanched or unblanched almonds in the microwave oven according to previous directions, adding 2 to 4 minutes. When nuts are golden, drizzle 2 teaspoons salad oil evenly over top, sprinkle with garlic salt mixture and stir well. Cook, uncovered, 2 to 3 minutes longer, stirring often, to blend flavors well.

Salted Peanuts. Spread 1 cup raw peanuts (with or without skins) in a single layer in a shallow dish. Cook, uncovered, in the microwave oven 6 to 8 minutes; stir once every minute. (Rub nuts between your hands to remove skins, if desired.) Drizzle 1 teaspoon salad oil evenly over nuts, sprinkle lightly with salt; stir well. Cook, uncovered, 45 seconds to 1 minute or until golden; stir every 15 seconds.

Mexican Peanuts. Stir together ¾ teaspoon chile powder, ½ teaspoon ground coriander, ¼ teaspoon *each* salt and ground cumin, and ⅛ teaspoon cayenne; set aside.

Roast 1 cup peanuts in the microwave oven following previous directions for Salted Peanuts. Omit salt and stir in chile powder mixture. Cook, uncovered, 2 minutes, stirring often, to blend flavors well.

Curried Peanuts. Stir together 1 teaspoon curry powder, ½ teaspoon seasoned salt, and ⅛ teaspoon garlic powder; set aside.

Roast 1 cup blanched or unblanched peanuts in the microwave oven following previous directions for Salted Peanuts. Omit salt and stir in curry mixture. Cook, uncovered, 1 to 2 minutes longer, stirring often to blend flavors well.

Salted Cashews. Roast 1 cup raw cashews in the microwave oven, following previous directions for Salted Peanuts but increasing the initial cooking time to about 12 minutes.

Cashews with Sansho Pepper. Roast 1 cup raw cashews in the microwave oven, following previous directions for Salted Peanuts but increasing the initial cooking time to about 12 minutes.

Then drizzle evenly with the 1 teaspoon salad oil plus 1 teaspoon sesame oil and cook, uncovered, 2 minutes longer (or until golden), stirring often. Sprinkle with about 1 teaspoon Sansho (Japanese pepper) and salt to taste.

Five-spice Cashews. Follow directions for Salted Cashews with Sansho Pepper. Instead of the Japanese pepper, use ½ teaspoon Chinese five-spice.

Pumpkin and Winter Squash Seeds. Rinse fibers from about 1 cup pumpkin seeds or Danish or butternut squash seeds (the shells are edible); drain. Sprinkle a light, even coating of salt in a shallow dish; arrange damp seeds in a single layer on the salt. Cook, uncovered, in the microwave oven 6 to 7 minutes or until seeds are crisp to bite; stir once every minute. (If you are toasting a smaller amount of seeds or if the seeds themselves are small, check for doneness after about 5 minutes.) Rub seeds between your fingers to remove excess salt before eating.

Roasted Sunflower Seeds. Follow previous directions for Pumpkin Seeds, using 1 cup hulled sunflower seeds. Cook, uncovered, in the microwave oven 5 minutes or until crisp to bite.

Mexican Sunflower Seeds. Prepare chile powder mixture following previous directions for Mexican Peanuts. Spread 1 cup hulled sunflower seeds in a single layer in a shallow baking dish. Cook, uncovered, in the microwave oven 5 minutes or until crisp; stir often. Drizzle with 1 teaspoon salad oil and sprinkle with the chile powder mixture. Cook, uncovered, 1 minute longer or until flavor is evenly distributed; stir once or twice.

Spiced Pecans. Roast 1 cup pecans in the microwave oven, following previous directions for Salted Peanuts but increasing the salad oil to 1 tablespoon.

Meanwhile, in a bag combine ½ cup sifted powdered sugar and 1½ teaspoons *each* ground cinnamon, ground cloves, and ground nutmeg. Add hot roasted nuts and shake well until heavily coated. Carefully lift out nuts and spread out to cool completely. Then place in a wire strainer and shake gently to remove excess sugar. Store any remaining sugar to use on other nuts, if desired.

Spiced Filberts. Roast 1 cup filberts in the microwave oven, following previous directions for Salted Peanuts but increasing the initial roasting time to about 12 minutes and the salad oil to 2 teaspoons. Follow preceding directions given for Spiced Pecans.

Salted Walnuts. To remove the astringent flavor of walnuts, bring 1½ cups water to a boil in a 1-quart glass measure or deep bowl in the microwave oven. Add 1 cup walnuts halves or pieces and boil, uncovered, 3 minutes. Drain, rinse under cold running water, spread out in a single layer on a towel, and let stand 15 minutes to dry. Then roast, following the directions for Salted Peanuts.

Smoky Walnuts. Stir together ¼ teaspoon *each* smoke-flavored salt and seasoned salt, ⅛ teaspoon *each* garlic powder, onion powder, and savory leaves, and dash cayenne. Set aside.

Prepare and roast walnuts in the microwave oven following previous directions for Salted Walnuts, increasing salad oil to 2 teaspoons. Omit salt and stir in smoke-flavored mixture. Cook, uncovered, 2 minutes or until flavor is evenly distributed, stirring often.

Parmesan Walnuts. Stir together 1 tablespoon grated Parmesan cheese, ½ teaspoon garlic salt, and ¼ teaspoon paprika; set aside.

Prepare and roast walnuts in the microwave oven, following previous directions for Salted Walnuts but increasing salad oil to 2 teaspoons. Omit salt and stir in cheese mixture. Cook, uncovered, 2 minutes or until flavor is evenly distributed, stirring often.

Garlic Butter Appetizers

The same garlic-flavored butter you can use for escargots is worth having on hand to season a number of other foods. Prepare the butter (you should have about ⅔ cup); keep it covered in the refrigerator as long as 2 to 3 weeks. Use in any of the recipes that follow and accompany with cubes of French bread to sop up the melted butter that remains in the serving dish.

½ cup (¼ lb.) butter, at room temperature
1 tablespoon finely chopped shallots
3 large cloves garlic, minced or pressed
2 tablespoons finely chopped parsley
Dash pepper

Blend butter, shallots, garlic, parsley, and pepper thoroughly; then cover and chill. Use in recipes below. Makes about ⅔ cup flavored butter.

Escargots. Snail shells (as well as the porcelain simulations found in cookware shops) make natural cooking containers for escargots. Or if you prefer, just cook the snails together in a small dish with the garlic butter, then serve on plates.

Drain 1 can (4½ oz.) snails (about 2 dozen) and place each in a natural or porcelain snail shell. With a small spoon, divide Garlic Butter mixture evenly among the shells, pressing smooth at shell opening. Arrange filled shells, open ends up, in four individual serving dishes, using either ceramic snail plates or shallow ramekins. (Or place butter mixture and snails in a small, shallow baking dish to heat.) Cover lightly with paper toweling and cook in the microwave oven 2 to 3 minutes, turning plates once or twice until butter bubbles vigorously. Serve with small forks or cocktail picks for spearing snails. Accompany with French bread to dip into garlic butter. Makes 4 servings, about 6 snails each.

Mushroom Caps. Select mushrooms about 1 inch in diameter; allow about 4 per person. Rinse, pat dry, and remove stems (reserve for other uses). Fill hollow of each mushroom with about ¼ teaspoon Garlic Butter, and arrange, cupped side up, in a rimmed serving dish. Cook 1 to 2 dozen mushrooms at a time, uncovered, in the microwave oven 2 to 4 minutes or until mushrooms are hot through and butter is bubbly; turn dish around once or twice during cooking. Let stand, covered, for 3 minutes. Serve with wooden picks.

Sliced Zucchini. Slice medium-size zucchini about ¼ inch thick, allowing 4 to 6 slices per person. Top each slice with about ¼ teaspoon Garlic Butter, sprinkle with paprika, and arrange slices side-by-side in a rimmed serving dish. Cook 1 to 2 dozen slices at a time, uncovered, in the microwave oven for 2 to 4 minutes or until zucchini is just tender when pierced; turn dish around once or twice during cooking. Let stand, covered, about 3 minutes. Serve with wooden picks for spearing.

Bite-size Meatballs. Prepare basic meatball recipe on page 28. Shape about 1½ teaspoons of the meat mixture around ¼ teaspoon Garlic Butter, completely sealing the butter. Arrange meatballs in a single layer in a rimmed serving dish. (Cover and refrigerate if made ahead.) Cook 1 to 2 dozen meatballs at a time, uncovered, in the microwave oven 3 to 5 minutes or until meat is no longer pink in center when slashed; turn dish once or twice during cooking. Garnish with chopped parsley and offer wooden picks for spearing. Makes about 4 dozen appetizers.

Sweet and Sour Cocktail Franks

When a sweet and sour sauce cooks in the microwave oven, there's little chance of its sticking to the bottom of the pot. Here, sliced frankfurters (or miniature frankfurters) are heated in the sauce. You can use the same sauce for cooked bite-size meatballs. Serve with wooden picks.

1½ teaspoons cornstarch
⅓ cup vinegar
¼ cup catsup
1 can (8 oz.) pineapple chunks packed in unsweetened juice
½ cup firmly packed brown sugar
1½ teaspoons soy sauce
1 medium-size green pepper, seeded and cut in 1-inch chunks
1 package (1 lb.) all-beef frankfurters cut in ½-inch diagonal slices (or 1 lb. miniature frankfurters)

In a 1½-quart baking dish, mix cornstarch and vinegar until smooth. Stir in catsup. Drain pineapple, saving ¼ cup of the liquid. Set fruit aside. Stir liquid into catsup mixture with sugar and soy sauce. Cook in the microwave oven 4 minutes, uncovered, stirring once or twice. Add green pepper and cook, uncovered, 4 minutes more, stirring frequently until sauce is thickened and clear. Add frankfurter slices and pineapple chunks; cook, stirring occasionally, 3 to 4 minutes longer or until frankfurters are heated through. Serve warm with cocktail picks to spear. Makes 4 to 5 dozen appetizers.

Hot Drinks

The neat trick about hot beverages from the microwave oven is preparing them right in their serving containers. Cups, mugs, pitchers, punch bowls, stemmed ware (even brandy snifters)—made of pottery, china, glass, paper, heavy plastic—all work well.

From breakfast cocoa to after-dinner drinks, these beverages are ready in minutes. You can perk a pot of coffee early in the day and reheat it by the cup when needed. Or heat instant coffee in water until it's steaming hot. For tea, simply heat the water; then drop in a bag or ball of spiced tea and let steep.

Remember the microwave, too, when you'd just like a little bouillon to sip. Drop a bouillon cube or teaspoon of stock base in a cup of water; then heat and stir until dissolved and hot. Top with a slice of lemon for added zest.

Hot Cocoa

For each serving, combine in a mug or cup sweetened cocoa and milk in proportions suggested on package. Heat, uncovered, in the microwave oven 1½ minutes. Stir well. Float a marshmallow atop the cocoa and cook, uncovered, 20 seconds or until marshmallow puffs.

Warming Brandy to Flame

For each serving, place about 1½ ounces brandy in a small glass or brandy snifter. Heat, uncovered, in the microwave oven 10 seconds. Ignite to flame before serving.

Crimson Apple Glögg

Even though this nonalcoholic punch takes as long to make in the microwave oven as it does on top of the range, the advantage is being able to heat or reheat it right in the punch bowl.

2 quarts apple juice
1 quart cranberry juice cocktail
2 sticks (2 inches *each*) cinnamon
4 whole cloves
2 tablespoons lemon juice
Thin unpeeled orange slices

Combine apple juice, cranberry juice cocktail, cinnamon, and cloves in a 4-quart soup tureen or punch bowl. Cook, uncovered, in the microwave oven 18 to 20 minutes or until hot. Discard spices, stir in lemon juice, and garnish with orange slices. Makes about 3 quarts.

Mulled Cider

Savor this spicy apple drink after a day on the slopes or any other winter outing. Make ahead, or come home and prepare it in no time.

1 quart apple cider
3 tablespoons sugar
4 whole allspice
5 whole cloves
1 strip lemon peel (about 2 inches)
1 stick cinnamon (about 2 inches)
¼ cup light or dark rum (optional)

In a 1½-quart glass pitcher or bowl, combine cider, sugar, allspice, cloves, lemon peel, and cinnamon. Heat, uncovered, in the microwave oven 5 to 7 minutes or until steaming hot. Stir to dissolve sugar and then stir in rum, if used. Pour through a wire strainer into glass cups or mugs. Makes 4 to 6 servings.

Café au Lait

For each serving, combine 2 teaspoons instant coffee and ⅔ cup milk in a cup or mug. Heat, uncovered, in the microwave oven 1½ minutes or until hot. Add sugar to taste, if desired.

Irish Coffee

For each serving, combine 2 teaspoons sugar and ⅔ cup strong coffee (or 1 teaspoon instant coffee and ⅔ cup hot tap water) in an 8-ounce stemmed glass or mug. Heat, uncovered, in the microwave oven 1½ minutes or until piping hot. Stir in 1 to 1½ ounces Irish whiskey and top with a dollop of whipped cream.

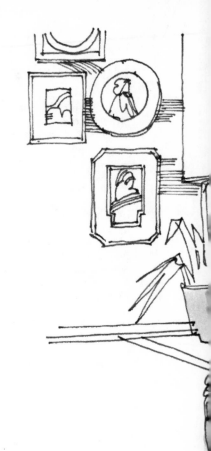

Soups

Savory first course or hearty full meal, cooked right in the bowl

The wizardry of microwave soup making can be easily explained—quick cooking keeps flavors fresh and intensifies color. And serving and cleanup are simplified because many soups cook in their serving containers.

All kinds of soups can be cooked electronically—light meal-starters to hearty full-meal entrées. But keep in mind that the volume of food in the oven determines how much time you save. Some soups take as long (or longer) to cook electronically as to cook conventionally; but color, flavor, easy cleanup, and a cool kitchen can be valid reasons for using the microwave oven. It's ideal for heating prepared soups or reheating your own homemade versions.

Your electric blender is a natural partner for microwave soups. Most of the chilled vegetable soups in this chapter make use of one. And since vegetables do retain their beautiful colors, the result is a brilliant, smooth purée.

Still, it's wise to honor tradition by simmering some kinds of soup on the back of a conventional range. Homemade stock needs long, slow cooking to develop and blend flavors; bony, fibrous meats need time to become tender and succulent. Such soups, with their many ingredients, generally require a large kettle and a generous amount of liquid, both of which are impractical in electronic cooking.

French Onion Soup

Prepare the broth ahead for this savory classic; then in the microwave oven, briefly reheat individual servings topped with shredded Swiss cheese.

¼ cup butter or margarine
3 large onions, thinly sliced
2 teaspoons all-purpose flour
6 cups regular-strength beef broth or 6 bouillon cubes and 6 cups water
⅓ cup dry white wine
Salt and pepper to taste
Garlic powder
6 to 8 slices crusty French bread (each ½ inch thick), toasted and buttered
1 cup shredded Swiss chese

In a 2½ to 3-quart deep casserole dish or soup tureen, melt butter in the microwave oven 45 seconds. Add onions to butter and cook, covered, 20 minutes, stirring every 3 minutes. Stir in flour and cook, uncovered, 1 minute.

Stir in beef broth (or bouillon cubes and water), white wine, and salt and pepper to taste. (Cover and refrigerate, if made ahead.) Cook, covered, 8 minutes (about 15 to 18 minutes if refrigerated). Stir once or twice.

To serve, lightly sprinkle garlic powder on hot buttered toast. Place 1 slice in each soup bowl; ladle soup over toast. Cover toast generously with cheese. Place 2 or 3 bowls at a time in oven. Cook, uncovered, until cheese melts (about 1 minute). Makes 6 to 8 servings.

Corn and Sausage Chowder

Fully cooked sausages team up with a few pantry shelf supplies to short-cut the preparation of this hearty soup.

1 pound Polish sausages or garlic frankfurters
1 medium-size onion, chopped
1 small potato, peeled and diced
½ cup hot water
1 can (12 oz.) whole kernel corn with red and green peppers
1 can (10¾ oz.) condensed cream of celery soup
1¼ cups milk
1 can (2¼ oz.) sliced ripe olives, drained
¼ teaspoon ground cumin
Salt and pepper

Thinly slice the sausage and put in a 3-quart soup tureen or casserole. Cover and cook in the microwave oven for 2 minutes, stirring once. Lift out sausages and set aside. Add onion to drippings and cook, covered, 2 minutes. Stir in potato and water and cook, covered, about 8 minutes or until potato is tender when pierced. Stir once or twice.

Stir in corn and any liquid, as well as soup, milk, olives, cumin, sausages, and salt and pepper to taste. Cover and cook 4 to 5 minutes or until hot; stir 2 or 3 times. Makes about 2 quarts.

Ravioli Soup

Stuffed pasta makes an interesting addition to this vegetable soup, and ravioli sauce from the can helps season the broth.

¾ cup each finely diced carrot and potato
3 cups hot water
¼ cup each thinly sliced green onion and chopped parsley
1 cup tomato juice
1 can (10½ oz.) condensed beef consommé
1 teaspoon sugar
¼ teaspoon pepper
1 can (about 15 oz.) ravioli
1 cup chopped spinach
Salt to taste
Grated Parmesan cheese

In a 3-quart soup tureen or casserole, combine carrot, potato, and 1 cup of the water. Cover and cook in the microwave oven 10 to 12 minutes or until vegetables are tender when pierced. Stir in the onion, parsley, tomato juice, consommé, sugar, and pepper. Cover and bring to boiling; stir in remaining 2 cups hot water, ravioli (including sauce), and spinach. Cover and cook 5 minutes or until piping hot, stirring once or twice. Season to taste with salt. Pass cheese at the table to sprinkle over top. Makes about 2 quarts.

Spicy Sausage Soup

Sausages supply the seasoning for this speedy main-dish soup. Using a canned soup as a base cuts preparation time.

About 12 ounces chorizo or linguisa
    sausages
Hot water
½ pound spinach
2 tablespoons butter or margarine
1 medium-size onion, chopped
1 can (10¾ oz.) condensed cream of
    potato soup
2 beef bouillon cubes

Place sausage links in a 2½-quart casserole or soup tureen; add about ½ inch hot water, cover, and cook in the microwave oven for 5 minutes; turn sausages over once or twice. Lift sausage out, thinly slice, and set aside. Discard drippings and wipe casserole clean.

Meanwhile, remove and discard spinach stems; rinse leaves well, drain, and coarsely chop. Set aside. Melt butter in casserole for 30 seconds; stir in onion and cook, covered, 4 minutes, stirring once. Stir in potato soup. Dissolve bouillon cubes in 2 cups hot water and stir into onion mixture with spinach and sausages. Cover and cook about 4 minutes, stirring once or twice until soup is hot through. Makes about 6 cups.

Sweet and Sour Bean Soup

Pantry shelf items, such as canned beans and stewed tomatoes, merge into this very mellow, well-blended soup. It's a good choice for lunch on a busy day.

6 slices bacon, diced
1 small onion, chopped
1 clove garlic, minced or pressed
1 can (about 14 oz.) stewed tomatoes
2 cans (about 16 oz. *each*) red kidney beans
1 teaspoon chile powder
¼ teaspoon *each* thyme leaves and dry basil
2 tablespoons red wine vinegar

Place bacon in a 3-quart soup tureen or casserole. Cover and cook about 5 minutes in the microwave oven until crisp; stir several times. With a slotted spoon, lift out bacon; drain. Discard all but 2 tablespoons of the drippings, add onion and garlic and cook, covered, 4 minutes or until limp. Stir in tomatoes, beans and their liquid, chile powder, thyme, and basil. Cover and cook 8 to 10 minutes or until piping hot; stir several times.

Remove about 1 cup of the beans, mash with a fork, and return to the soup tureen to slightly thicken the soup. Stir in vinegar and bacon. Makes about 2 quarts.

Mushroom Velvet Soup

For an easy picnic idea, pack soup along in a vacuum bottle. You can serve it either chilled or reheated, depending on the weather.

¼ cup butter or margarine
½ pound mushrooms, sliced
1 medium-size onion, chopped
1 cup chopped parsley, lightly packed
1 tablespoon all-purpose flour
1 can (14 oz.) regular-strength beef broth
1 cup sour cream

In a 7 by 11-inch baking dish, melt butter 30 seconds in the microwave oven. Add mushrooms, onion, and parsley and cook, uncovered, 5 minutes, stirring once or twice. Stir in flour and add ½ cup of the beef broth. Cook, uncovered, about 1 minute or until bubbly.

In a blender, whirl vegetable mixture, a portion at a time, with sour cream and the remaining beef broth until smooth (or force through a food mill). If made ahead, cover and chill. Serve cold or reheat, covered, 3 minutes in the microwave oven. Sip from glasses or cups. Makes 4 servings.

Minestrone Presto

Lots of colorful vegetables go into this Italian soup. You can easily turn it into a hearty one-dish meal by adding about 3 cups cooked meat or poultry.

2 small potatoes, scrubbed
1 tablespoon olive oil or salad oil
1 medium-size onion, finely chopped
2 large carrots, shredded
½ cup chopped celery
1 can (14½ oz.) sliced baby tomatoes
1 can (15 oz.) pinto beans
3 cups hot water
2 tablespoons beef stock base or 6 beef
    bouillon cubes
1 medium-size zucchini, thinly sliced
1 cup frozen cut green beans, thawed
1 cup coarsely chopped spinach or Swiss
    chard leaves
Green Sauce (recipe follows)
Salt and pepper to taste
Shredded Parmesan cheese

Pierce unpeeled potatoes several times with a fork. Cook in the microwave oven, uncovered, 6 minutes or until soft when squeezed, turning once; set aside.

(Continued on next page)

In a 4-quart soup tureen or casserole, mix oil, onion, carrots, and celery. Cover and cook 8 minutes until vegetables are almost soft. Meanwhile, peel cooked potatoes and cut into ½-inch cubes. Stir potatoes, tomatoes and their liquid, pinto beans and their liquid, water, and beef stock base into onion mixture. Cook, covered, 12 minutes or until liquid boils, stirring 2 or 3 times. Mix in zucchini, green beans, and spinach. Cover and cook 10 minutes until vegetables are almost tender when pierced. Stir well and let stand, covered, for 5 minutes. Stir Green Sauce into soup. Add salt and pepper to taste. Pass cheese to sprinkle over each serving. Makes 6 to 8 servings.

Green Sauce. In a small bowl, mix 1 tablespoon olive oil or salad oil with 1 clove garlic (minced or pressed), ¼ cup chopped parsley, and 1 tablespoon dry basil. Cover and heat until parsley is wilted (about 1 minute).

French Country Vegetable Soup

Imagine a wintertime soup simmering away in an old cast iron kettle on the back of a country stove in France. Now in minutes you can have the same soup—one that retains the color and remarkably fresh flavor of vegetables. Some variations follow under the heading Country Greens Soup.

- 2 tablespoons butter or margarine
- 2 bunches green onions, thinly sliced, including part of tops
- 1 small onion, sliced
- 1 cup chopped celery
- 1 large carrot, shredded (about 1 cup)
- 1 medium-size turnip, peeled and cubed
- 1 large potato, peeled and cubed
- 2 cans (about 14 oz. *each*) regular-strength chicken broth
- ¼ teaspoon marjoram leaves
  Salt and pepper

In a 3-quart casserole dish, melt butter in the microwave oven 1 minute. Stir in green onion, onion, celery, and carrot. Cover and cook until celery begins to soften (about 10 minutes). Mix in turnip, potato, and ¼ cup of the broth. Cover and cook 13 minutes, stirring 2 or 3 times until potato is tender when pierced. Stir in remaining chicken broth and marjoram. Whirl about a third of the mixture at a time in a blender, transferring each portion of the puréed soup to a tureen or serving bowl. Add salt and pepper to taste. Cover and reheat the soup 5 to 8 minutes to serving temperature. Makes 4 to 6 servings.

Country Greens Soup

Follow the previous recipe for French Country Vegetable Soup, omitting the turnip and potato. Instead, substitute 3 cups coarsely chopped spinach or Swiss chard leaves; or 1 package (10 oz.) frozen chopped broccoli (thawed); or 3 small zucchini, thinly sliced. Add after celery mixture is cooked. Continue cooking, covered, 1½ minutes for spinach; about 5 minutes for broccoli; about 8 minutes for zucchini. Omit blending. Stir in remaining broth and marjoram and heat, covered, 6 to 8 minutes or until hot. Just before serving, stir in 1 to 2 teaspoons lemon juice. Add salt and pepper to taste. Top each serving with a dollop of sour cream. Makes 4 to 6 servings.

Hearty Beef and Cabbage Soup

Cold winter nights call for hearty, hot soups. This one—chock full of meat and vegetables—goes well with hunks of French bread.

- 1 pound lean ground beef
- 1 medium-size onion, thinly sliced
- ½ cup thinly sliced celery
- 1 can (1 lb.) tomatoes
- 2 cups water
- 1 can (1 lb.) red kidney beans
- 1 teaspoon *each* salt and chile powder
- ⅛ teaspoon pepper
- 2 cups thinly shredded cabbage

In a soup tureen or casserole (at least 2½-quart size), cook the beef, uncovered, in the microwave oven 5 minutes, stirring often until crumbly. Add onion and celery and cook, covered, about 5 minutes; stir once. Discard any fat. Stir in tomatoes and their liquid (breaking up tomatoes with a fork), water, beans and their liquid, salt, chile powder, and pepper. Cover and bring to a boil (takes about 6 minutes). Add cabbage and cook, covered, 4 minutes or until cabbage is tender to bite. Serve in soup plates or bowls. Makes 4 to 6 servings.

Riviera Fish Soup

Dishes hailing from the French Riviera are often redolent of garlic and tomatoes. This soup is mildly seasoned with those traditional ingredients and can be put together with little effort. Serve with hot garlic French bread as a main course.

- 1 small onion, sliced
- 1 clove garlic, minced or pressed
- ¼ cup sliced celery
- 1 tablespoon olive oil or salad oil
- 2 tablespoons chopped parsley
- ½ teaspoon Italian herb seasoning or ⅛ teaspoon *each* dry basil, oregano, thyme, and marjoram leaves
    Dash cayenne
- 1 can (10¾ oz.) condensed tomato soup
- 2 tablespoons tomato paste
- 1¼ cups hot water
- 1 can (8 oz.) minced clams
- 1 can (4½ oz.) shrimp, drained and rinsed or ¼ pound small cooked and shelled shrimp
- 1 pound Greenland turbot or rockfish fillets, thawed if frozen
    Salt and pepper to taste

In a 2½ to 3-quart deep casserole or soup tureen, mix onion, garlic, celery, and olive oil. Cover and cook in the microwave oven 8 minutes or until celery is wilted, stirring 2 or 3 times. Add parsley, herb seasoning, cayenne, tomato soup, and tomato paste. Stir in water. Then stir in clams and their liquid and shrimp. Cut fish into 1½-inch-square pieces and mix into soup. Cover and cook 8 to 10 minutes or until liquid is piping hot and fish pieces are opaque and flake easily with a fork. Stir 3 or 4 times. Add salt and pepper to taste. Makes 4 main-dish servings.

Asparagus Clam Chowder

Fresh asparagus added to clam chowder makes it a distinctive luncheon or supper soup to serve with a meat or cheese sandwich.

- 2 tablespoons butter or margarine
- 1 small onion, chopped
- 1 medium-size potato, peeled and diced
- 1½ cups hot water
- 1 can (8 oz.) minced clams
- 1 pound asparagus
- 2 cups milk
- ½ teaspoon salt
- ¼ teaspoon pepper
- 2 tablespoons chopped parsley

Melt 1 tablespoon of the butter in a 2½-quart soup tureen or deep casserole for 30 seconds in the microwave oven. Add onion and cook 2½ minutes or until limp. Stir in the potato and 1 cup of the water. Drain clam broth into casserole (reserving clams); cover and cook 6 minutes or until potatoes are tender when pierced.

Meanwhile, snap off and discard white fibrous ends from asparagus; rinse spears and cut slanting slices about 1 inch long. Add to potato mixture along with the remaining ½ cup water. Continue to cook, uncovered, until asparagus is just tender when pierced (about 6 minutes), stirring once. Stir in clams, milk, remaining 1 tablespoon butter, salt, and pepper. Cook, covered, 1½ minutes or until hot through; do not boil. Stir in parsley and serve at once. Makes 6 servings.

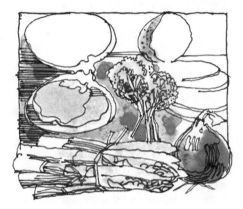

Iced Carrot and Orange Soup

A smooth, golden blend of carrot and fresh orange can spark appetites when offered as a soup before lunch or dinner.

- 2 tablespoons butter or margarine
- 1 large onion, sliced
- 1 pound carrots, thinly sliced
- 3 cups regular-strength chicken broth
- 1 teaspoon sugar
- ½ teaspoon dill weed
- 1½ cups freshly squeezed orange juice
    Salt to taste

In the microwave oven, melt butter in a 2 to 2½-quart baking dish for 30 seconds. Add onion, cover, and cook 2 minutes. Add carrots, about half the broth, the sugar, and dill weed. Cover and cook 11 minutes or until carrots are very tender when pierced. Add remaining broth.

Whirl half the mixture at a time in a blender until smooth. Stir in orange juice. Season to taste with salt. Cover and chill. Makes about 6½ cups.

Chilled Beet Soup

Magenta-colored and satin-textured, this soup is a blend of beets and tangy buttermilk with a hint of dill. Accent each serving with crunchy apple bits.

    6 cups peeled, diced beets (about 7
        medium size)
    2 cans (about 14 oz. *each*) regular-strength
        chicken broth
    2 cups buttermilk
    1 teaspoon dill weed
      Salt and pepper
    ¾ cup thinly sliced green onion
    1 large apple
    2 teaspoons lemon juice
      Sour cream

Put beets in a 3-quart baking dish, add ½ cup of the broth, cover, and cook 20 minutes in the microwave oven or until tender when pierced; stir several times. Add remaining broth.

Whirl half of the mixture at a time in a blender until smooth. Stir in buttermilk, dill, salt and pepper to taste, and onion. Cover and chill thoroughly. To serve, pour into a serving bowl. Core and dice the apple and mix well with lemon juice. Pass apple and sour cream. Makes 10 cups.

Avocado Madrilene

Diced avocado dots this colorful, jellied tomato-beef madrilene. Make it ahead as an elegant opener to lunch or dinner.

    1 envelope unflavored gelatin
    2 cups vegetable juice cocktail
    1 can (10½ oz.) condensed beef broth
    1 tablespoon Worcestershire
      Liquid hot pepper seasoning to taste
    1 large avocado
    ¾ cup sour cream
    ½ cup thinly sliced green onion

Sprinkle gelatin over the vegetable juice cocktail in a 2½-cup bowl or dish. Let stand 5 minutes. Cover and cook in the microwave oven 2½ minutes to dissolve gelatin. Then combine with beef broth and Worcestershire. Season with hot pepper seasoning and chill until syrupy (about 20 minutes).

Spoon soup into 6 to 8 shallow bowls. Halve and peel avocado, then dice. Divide avocado equally among bowls; stir gently to submerge avocado. Chill until set. Top each serving with sour cream and green onion. Makes 6 to 8 servings.

Chilled Vegetable Bisque

A generous amount of watercress gives spritely tang to this smooth vegetable purée. Garnish soup with some sliced green onion and crisp, crumbled bacon.

    1½ cups diced carrots
     2 cups thinly sliced leeks
     2 cups peeled, diced new potatoes
     2 cans (about 14 oz. *each*) regular-strength
        chicken broth
     1 cup chopped watercress, loosely packed
    ½ to ¾ cup milk
       Salt, pepper, and ground nutmeg
       Thinly sliced green onion
       Crisply cooked bacon, crumbled (or
         bacon-flavored chips)

In a 3-quart casserole, combine carrots, leeks, potatoes, and 1 can of the chicken broth. Cover and cook in the microwave oven 12 to 14 minutes; stir several times. Add watercress and cook, covered, 2 minutes. Stir in remaining broth.

Whirl a small amount of the mixture at a time in a blender until smooth. Stir in enough milk to thin to desired consistency; season to taste with salt, pepper, and nutmeg. Cover and chill thoroughly. Serve, topped with green onion and bacon. Makes 7 cups.

Curried Broccoli Soup

Cool, green broccoli purée comes alive with a nip of curry. Serve as an inviting meal opener or lunchtime treat. Garnish with lightly cooked broccoli flowerets and chopped salted peanuts.

    2 pounds broccoli (about 2 bunches)
    2 cans (about 14 oz. *each*) regular-strength
        chicken broth
    3 tablespoons butter or margarine
    2 medium-size onions, chopped
    1½ teaspoons curry powder
      Sour cream
      Chopped salted peanuts

Trim tough stem ends from broccoli. Cut off the flowerets in bite-size pieces. Also coarsely chop stems; set aside.

Place about half of the flowerets in a 3-quart dish with ½ cup of broth; cover and cook 3 minutes in the microwave oven or until just tender when pierced. Lift out broccoli, cool, cover, and chill.

Add butter, onion, and curry to dish; cover and cook 3 minutes. Stir in broccoli stems, remaining flowerets, and ½ cup of broth. Cover; cook 10 minutes or until tender when pierced. Add remaining broth.

Whirl part of the mixture at a time in a blender until smooth. Cover and chill.

To serve, ladle into small bowls and top with cooked flowerets. Pass sour cream and peanuts. Makes 7 cups.

Cool Golden Chowder

Make this mellow potpourri of golden carrots, squash, and corn as far in advance as two days. Serve accompanied with salted sunflower seeds and a garnish of parsley.

- **2 tablespoons butter or margarine**
- **1 medium-size onion, chopped**
- **1 cup chopped carrot**
- **2½ cups chopped crookneck squash**
- **1 can (about 14 oz.) regular-strength chicken broth**
- **1 cup corn, cut from cob**
- **¼ teaspoon thyme leaves**
- **Salt and pepper**
- **½ cup milk**
- **Chopped parsley**
- **Salted sunflower seeds**

Melt butter in a 2 to 2½-quart baking dish 30 seconds in the microwave oven. Add onion, cover, and cook 2 minutes. Stir in carrot, squash, and ½ cup of the broth; cover and cook 5 minutes. Add corn, cover, and cook 8 minutes longer or until vegetables are tender when pierced. Add remaining broth.

Whirl about half of the mixture at a time in blender until smooth. Add thyme and salt and pepper to taste. Cover and chill. To serve, stir in milk, garnish with parsley. Pass salted sunflower seeds to sprinkle over servings. Makes about 5 cups.

Heating Prepared Soups

Using convenient prepared soups in conjunction with the microwave is an energy saver for both you and your oven.

Mix-in-a-cup Soup. Measure ¾ cup hot water (or amount specified on package) into a cup or mug. Heat in the microwave oven 2 minutes or until water boils. Slowly stir in 1 packet (¼ of a 6-oz. package) dry soup mix. Stir until dissolved.

Dry Soup. In a 2-quart soup tureen or casserole, stir together 1 package or envelope soup mix (amount for 4 to 6 servings) and 4 cups hot water (or amount specified on package). Cover and cook in the microwave oven about 10 minutes or until liquid is bubbling all over the surface. Let stand, covered, 2 to 3 minutes. Stir well before serving. Makes 4 to 6 servings.

Canned Soup. For a single serving of *condensed soup*, fill a mug or bowl a little less than half full with soup; gradually stir in an equal quantity of hot tap water. Cook, uncovered, in the microwave oven 2 to 3 minutes or until hot and bubbly. One can makes 2 or 3 servings.

To prepare an entire can of condensed soup, spoon soup into a small deep casserole (about 1 qt. size); gradually stir in an equal quantity of hot tap water and cook, covered, 6 to 8 minutes or until hot and bubbly.

For *heat-and-eat canned soup* (regular-strength), simply heat, uncovered, in individual containers or a small casserole; times will be about the same as for condensed soups given above.

Pouch-packed Frozen Soup. Place an 8-ounce pouch of frozen soup in a 1½-quart casserole. Pierce top with a fork in 3 or 4 places. Cook, uncovered, in the microwave oven 5 minutes or until hot and bubbling in center. Cut open one corner of pouch and pour into bowl. Serves 1.

Meats

Microwave methods
for beef, pork, lamb, veal

Microwave meat cookery is serious business. Tender roasts of beef, pork, lamb, and veal are fine candidates. Ground meats (patties, casseroles, meatloaf) and precooked meats, such as ham and sausage, do equally well.

But meats that you would normally braise or simmer for long periods, such as Swiss steak or corned beef, are best cooked in the conventional way unless your microwave oven has a LOW POWER/DEFROST setting or variable control (see descriptions on pages 5-6) for slow cooking. Some recipes in this chapter call for this setting.

Roasts that fare best when cooked electronically are tender cuts popularly known as "oven roasts." They are compactly shaped, weigh at least 3 pounds, have surface fat trimmed to a minimum, and are tied securely if boned and rolled.

While cooking, a roast should be elevated in its baking dish on a nonmetallic rack made for microwave ovens (or on an inverted saucer) so it won't sit and stew in its own drippings. Turning the roast over once or twice makes for more even cooking.

Salting a roast before cooking draws out the juices and may account for some surface toughening, so add salt when meat is done. Pepper, a rubbing of fresh garlic (or garlic powder), paprika, or herbs can be used freely on uncooked meat.

Ground meats are already tender and take very little cooking time—just enough to lose pinkness. Buy lean ground meats to avoid fat accumulation when cooking. Cook meat patties elevated on a nonmetallic rack made for microwave ovens, if you have one. Or use one of the special browning utensils (see page 7) made for microwave use.

For steaks and chops, use your conventional broiler or barbecue if you like a browned exterior and pink-rare interior. Or use one

of the special browning utensils mentioned above.

The lack of browning that is characteristic of microwave cooking can be overcome in several ways. Some manufacturers have installed a browning unit that operates independently from the microwave action. But if your oven has no such unit, you can use the broiler of your conventional oven.

To give the meat surface a browned appearance while adding color and flavor, apply a sauce or baste. We suggest several in our recipes. Or you can try soy, Worcestershire, teriyaki, or bottled brown gravy sauce.

Time required for cooking meats will vary, depending on the size of the meat cut, the temperature of the meat before cooking, how well-done you like it, and your particular oven. The manufacturer's manual generally includes several cooking time charts. Refer to them as a guide for cooking meats in your particular oven.

Like other microwave-cooked foods, meats continue to cook after they have been removed from the oven. We recommend undercooking and then using the "standing time" (see page 7) outside the oven to finish the cooking.

After the meat has cooked for the estimated time, take it out of the oven and insert a standard meat thermometer. Let stand about 10 minutes to register the internal temperature. If more time is needed, remove the thermometer and return the meat to the oven. Never use a thermometer in your oven unless it's the kind made especially for your type of microwave oven.

Some newer ovens have a built-in heat sensing device. It's inserted into the meat before cooking and automatically shuts off the oven when the desired temperature is reached.

Basic Meatballs

For party appetizers (see page 16) or a family dinner, try this simple meatball recipe or one of the variations that follow.

    1 egg, slightly beaten
    ¼ cup tomato juice
    1 teaspoon Worcestershire
    ½ cup soft bread crumbs
    1 pound lean ground beef
    ¼ cup finely chopped onion
    1 teaspoon salt
    ⅛ teaspoon pepper

Mix together egg, tomato juice, and Worcestershire. Add bread crumbs and let stand a few minutes. Thoroughly mix in ground beef, onion, salt, and pepper. Shape into 1½-inch balls. Arrange in a single layer in a 9-inch-square baking dish. Cook, uncovered, in the microwave oven 6 to 10 minutes or until no longer pink when slashed. Reposition inside meatballs to the edges of dish once during cooking (meatballs along edges will cook fastest). Turn dish around several times. Drain and discard drippings. Serves 4.

Italian Meatballs. Prepare and cook Basic Meatballs (see preceding recipe), decreasing salt to ½ teaspoon and lightly mixing in ⅓ cup shredded Parmesan cheese, 2 tablespoons chopped parsley, and about half of a 1½-ounce package spaghetti sauce mix; reserve the remainder. When cooked, remove meatballs with a slotted spoon and set aside.

Skim and discard fat from drippings in baking dish; then add remaining spaghetti sauce mix, ¾ cup hot water, and 1 can (8 oz.) tomato sauce; stir until smooth. Cook, uncovered, 8 to 10 minutes until bubbling and slightly thickened, stirring 2 or 3 times. Return meatballs to baking dish. Spoon sauce over them. Cover and cook 2 to 3 minutes or until heated through. Serve over hot cooked spaghetti and top with additional shredded Parmesan cheese. Makes 4 servings.

Curried Meatballs. Prepare and cook Basic Meatballs (see preceding recipe), mixing in ¼ teaspoon garlic powder with the seasonings called for. When cooked, remove meatballs with a slotted spoon and set aside.

Skim fat from drippings in dish and discard. To the remaining drippings, stir in 1½ teaspoons all-purpose flour, 1½ teaspoons curry powder, dash cayenne, 2 green onions (thinly sliced), and ½ cup *each* regular-strength chicken broth and half-and-half (light cream). Cook, uncovered, 4 to 7 minutes until bubbling and thickened, stirring

2 or 3 times. Add salt to taste. Return meatballs to baking dish and spoon sauce over them. Cover and cook 2 to 3 minutes or until heated through. Serve with hot cooked rice and accompany with chutney, chopped cucumber, and chopped salted peanuts or almonds. Makes 4 servings.

Porcupine Meatballs. Prepare Basic Meatballs (see preceding recipe), mixing in 1 cup quick-cooking rice. Shape into 12 equal meatballs and place in a 9-inch-square baking dish. Mix together ¼ cup chopped green pepper, 1 can (10¾ oz.) condensed tomato soup, ⅓ cup hot water, and ¼ teaspoon chile powder; pour over meatballs. Cover and cook 12 to 15 minutes until meatballs are no longer pink when slashed and rice is tender to bite, stirring and turning dish several times. Let stand, covered, 5 minutes. Serves 4.

Cheeseburger in a Bun

Cook the beef patties in the microwave oven; then assemble these all-American sandwiches to reheat when you need them.

    1 pound lean ground beef
    1 tablespoon chopped green onion
    ½ teaspoon salt
    ¼ teaspoon pepper
    2 tablespoons catsup
       Cheese Topping (recipe follows)
    4 hamburger buns, split and lightly
       buttered

Combine ground beef, onion, salt, pepper, and catsup; mix well and shape into 4 equal patties. Place in an 8-inch-square baking dish and cook, covered lightly, in the microwave oven 4 minutes for rare, or until done to your liking. Let cool while you prepare Cheese Topping.

Place each meat patty on a bun half; top with about a fourth of the Cheese Topping and remaining bun half. Enclose each bun tightly in plastic film and refrigerate as long as 24 hours.

To reheat, unwrap buns, place them on a serving platter, cover lightly with a paper towel, and heat all four in the microwave oven 2½ to 3 minutes or just until meat is hot through and Cheese Topping has melted. (Or heat each bun individually about 45 seconds.) Makes 4 servings.

Cheese Topping. Combine 1 cup shredded sharp Cheddar cheese, 2 tablespoons soft butter or margarine, 1½ teaspoons catsup, ½ teaspoon prepared mustard, and 1 tablespoon finely chopped green onion.

Grated Carrot Meat Loaf for a Crowd

A mustard-flavored sugary glaze bakes on this carrot-flecked ground beef loaf.

    2 slices firm white bread, broken in pieces
    ¾ cup milk
  2½ pounds lean ground beef
    3 eggs
    2 large carrots, finely shredded
    2 tablespoons prepared horseradish
    1 envelope (about 1½ oz.) onion soup mix
       (enough for 3 or 4 servings)
    ¼ cup catsup
    3 tablespoons firmly packed brown sugar
    2 tablespoons Dijon mustard

Whirl bread in a blender to make about 1 cup fine crumbs. In a large mixing bowl, pour milk over bread crumbs and let stand until absorbed. Mix in ground beef, eggs, carrots, horseradish, and onion soup mix. Pat into a 5 by 9-inch loaf pan. Mix together catsup, brown sugar, and mustard; spread evenly over the top. Cook, uncovered, in the microwave oven for about 25 minutes or until meat loaf is no longer pink in center when slashed; turn dish every 5 minutes. Let stand, covered, 5 minutes. Drain off accumulated juices before serving. Makes 8 to 10 servings.

Cottage Cheese Meat Loaf

Small nuggets of cottage cheese mixed with ground beef make an exceptionally moist and tender meat loaf.

    1 pound lean ground beef
    1 cup (½ pint) cottage cheese
    1 egg
    ½ cup quick-cooking rolled oats
    ¼ cup catsup
    1 tablespoon prepared mustard
    1 tablespoon instant minced onion
    ½ teaspoon salt
    ⅛ teaspoon pepper
    ⅓ cup grated Parmesan cheese

Combine ground beef with cottage cheese, egg, rolled oats, catsup, mustard, onion, salt, and pepper. Mix ingredients lightly until well blended. Press loosely into an 8-inch-square baking dish. Cook, uncovered, in the microwave oven 12 to 14 minutes, turning dish once. Sprinkle top of meat loaf with Parmesan cheese and cook 1½ minutes or until cheese is melted and meat is no longer pink when slashed. Let stand, covered, 5 minutes before serving. Cut in squares. Makes 4 servings.

Mushroom and Raisin Meat Loaf

Crisp bacon strips top this juicy meat loaf, and each slice is studded with chopped mushrooms and raisins.

    2 slices firm white bread
  1½ pounds lean ground beef
    ½ pound bulk sausage
    2 eggs
    2 tablespoons nonfat dry milk
    ¼ cup raisins
    2 cups coarsely chopped mushrooms (about ⅓ lb.)
    2 tablespoons Worcestershire
    1 teaspoon salt
    ½ teaspoon pepper
    3 strips bacon
    ¼ cup catsup

Whirl bread in a blender to make fine crumbs (you should have about 1 cup). Mix crumbs with beef, sausage, eggs, dry milk, raisins, mushrooms, Worcestershire, salt, and pepper. Press lightly into a 5 by 9-inch glass loaf pan.

Lay bacon strips between two paper towels in a baking dish (or place on a nonmetallic rack set in baking dish and cover with paper towel). Cook in the microwave oven 3 minutes. Drain bacon and place lengthwise on meat loaf. Drizzle catsup over bacon. Cook, uncovered, about 22 minutes or until meat is no longer pink when slashed. Let stand, covered, 5 minutes before serving. Makes 6 to 8 servings.

Use full power setting on all recipes unless otherwise indicated

Meats **29**

Sweet and Sour Beef

Crunchy green or red bell pepper chunks and sweet pineapple pieces make a colorful mixture that cooks together in one dish.

⅓ cup firmly packed brown sugar
2 tablespoons cornstarch
¼ cup red wine vinegar
3 tablespoons soy sauce
1 can (1 lb. 4 oz.) pineapple chunks or tidbits
1 pound lean ground beef
1 small green or red bell pepper, seeded and cut in thin strips
1 medium-size onion, sliced
   Hot cooked rice or noodles

Blend sugar, cornstarch, vinegar, and soy. Drain pineapple, reserving ¾ cup of the liquid. Blend liquid with sugar mixture. Set sauce and pineapple aside.

Crumble ground beef into a 3-quart baking dish. Cook, uncovered, in the microwave oven 4 to 5 minutes or until meat loses its pinkness. Stir in pepper and onion, cover, and cook 2 minutes. Stir in the sauce and cook, uncovered, 4 to 5 minutes or until thickened, stirring once or twice. Add pineapple and cook, uncovered, about 1½ minutes or until heated through. Serve with hot rice or noodles. Makes 4 servings.

Beef and Mushroom Bake

A bubbly cheese topping crowns this casserole of ground beef, spinach, and mushrooms.

2 packages (10 or 12 oz. *each*) frozen chopped spinach
1 pound lean ground beef
2 tablespoons butter or margarine
½ pound mushrooms, sliced
1 tablespoon instant minced onion
1 cup sour cream
1 teaspoon salt
½ teaspoon *each* oregano leaves, dry basil, and thyme leaves
⅛ teaspoon ground nutmeg
1 cup *each* shredded Cheddar and grated Parmesan cheese

Cook unwrapped packages of frozen spinach in the microwave oven 3 minutes until slightly thawed (or turn spinach into a wire strainer and rinse with hot water until thawed). Press out all the water from spinach; set aside.

Crumble ground beef into a 7 by 11-inch baking dish and cook, uncovered, 5 minutes or until meat loses pinkness; drain off drippings and set meat aside.

In the same dish, melt butter 30 seconds. Add mushrooms and onion and cook, covered, 4 minutes, stirring once.

Stir in meat, spinach, sour cream, salt, oregano, basil, thyme, nutmeg, and ½ cup each of the Cheddar and Parmesan cheese. Sprinkle remaining cheese over top. Bake, uncovered, for 7½ minutes or until heated through; turn dish once or twice. Makes 6 servings.

Lasagne Belmonte

Three kinds of cheese are interspersed among layers of wide lasagne noodles and a thick tomato meat sauce. Noodles cook just as fast on top of your conventional range. They can be cooking while you prepare the rest of the casserole.

½ package (10-oz. size) lasagne noodles
   Boiling water
1 tablespoon olive oil or salad oil
1 small onion, chopped
1 small clove garlic, minced or pressed
1 pound lean ground beef
1 can (8 oz.) tomato sauce
½ can (6-oz. size) tomato paste
¼ cup *each* dry red wine and water (or ½ cup water)
   Salt
½ teaspoon oregano leaves
¼ teaspoon *each* pepper and sugar
1 cup ricotta cheese or small curd cottage cheese
¼ pound mozzarella cheese, thinly sliced
¼ cup shredded Parmesan cheese

Cook noodles in boiling water on top of your conventional range, following package directions; drain well, rinse with cold water, then drain again.

Meanwhile, in a 7 by 11-inch baking dish, place oil, onion, and garlic. Cook, uncovered, in the microwave oven 3 to 4 minutes or until onion is soft, stirring twice. Add ground beef and cook, uncovered, 3 minutes, stirring every minute until meat loses pinkness; drain off fat. Stir in tomato sauce, tomato paste, wine, and water. Add salt to taste, oregano, pepper, and sugar, stirring until mixed. Cook, uncovered, 2 minutes. Remove to another dish.

In the baking dish the meat sauce cooked in, arrange about half the drained noodles to almost make a solid layer. Spread half the tomato sauce over noodles; top with half the ricotta and mozzarella cheese. Repeat layering and top with Parmesan (can be refrigerated if made ahead).

Cook, uncovered, 4 to 5 minutes (6 minutes, if refrigerated) or until cheese melts, and mixture is heated through; turn dish once or twice. Makes 5 or 6 servings.

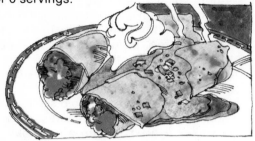

Beef and Bean Enchiladas

Tortillas can be softened quickly in the microwave oven, eliminating the messy job of heating them in oil. You can put these enchiladas together up to a day ahead and then reheat to serve. Pass the sour cream and chile salsa.

    1 tablespoon butter or margarine
    1 small onion, chopped
    ¾ pound lean ground beef, crumbled
    ½ can (1-lb. size) refried beans
    ½ teaspoon salt
    ⅛ teaspoon garlic powder
    2½ tablespoons prepared red taco sauce
    ½ cup quartered pitted ripe olives
    1 can (10 oz.) enchilada sauce
    6 corn tortillas
    1½ cups shredded Cheddar cheese
      Sliced pitted ripe olives for garnish
      Sour cream
      Canned green chile salsa

In a 7 by 11-inch baking dish, melt butter in the microwave oven 30 seconds. Add onion and cook, uncovered, 4 minutes, stirring once or twice. Add meat to dish and cook, uncovered, 5 minutes, stirring often. Discard any accumulated fat. Stir in beans, salt, garlic powder, taco sauce, and ½ cup olives. Cook, uncovered, 4½ minutes until beans start to bubble around edges of dish; stir once. If you don't have another 7 by 11-inch baking dish, transfer beef-bean mixture to another container. Wash baking dish and then pour in enchilada sauce. Heat, uncovered, 2 minutes, stirring once.

Wrap tortillas in plastic film and heat 45 seconds. Place about ⅓ cup of the beef filling on each tortilla and roll to enclose filling. Roll filled tortillas over in hot enchilada sauce, placing seam sides down in a single layer in sauce.

Spoon sauce over top to moisten all surfaces. Sprinkle with Cheddar cheese. Cover and cook 3½ minutes or until heated through and cheese is melted; turn dish once. (Or cover and refrigerate for up to 1 day; if taken directly from refrigerator, increase baking time to 6 minutes.) Garnish with olive slices. Spoon sour cream and chile salsa over each serving to taste. Makes 3 servings of 2 enchiladas each.

Athenian Moussaka

You cook all the elements for this entrée in sequence right in the same baking dish; then use the dish to assemble, bake, and serve moussaka.

    1 small eggplant (about 1 lb.)
      About ¼ cup olive oil or salad oil
      Meat Sauce (recipe follows)
      Custard Topping (recipe follows)
    ¼ cup grated Parmesan cheese
      Ground nutmeg

Trim stem end from eggplant and cut lengthwise in ¼-inch slices. Pour about 3 tablespoons oil into a 7 by 11-inch baking dish; turn eggplant slices in the oil to coat both sides, adding more oil if necessary. In the dish, arrange as many slices as will fit in a single layer; cover and cook in the microwave oven 3 minutes. Turn eggplant slices over and cook 2 minutes or until soft. Lift out and set aside; repeat procedure with remaining eggplant, adding more oil if necessary.

Prepare the Meat Sauce and Custard Topping.

To assemble the casserole, arrange half the eggplant slices in the baking dish, spoon over Meat Sauce, and top with remaining eggplant. Pour on Custard Topping, sprinkle Parmesan cheese evenly over all, and then sprinkle with nutmeg. Cook, uncovered, 15 minutes or until custard is set; turn dish several times. Let stand, uncovered, about 5 minutes before serving. Makes about 6 servings.

Meat Sauce. Pour 1 tablespoon salad oil in the baking dish; add 1 medium-size onion (chopped) and cook, covered, 2 minutes; stir once. Distribute 1¼ pounds lean ground lamb or beef over onions. Cook, uncovered, about 6 minutes or until meat is crumbly; stir often. Stir in 1 teaspoon salt, 1 can (6 oz.) tomato paste, ½ cup dry red wine, 2 tablespoons finely chopped parsley, ½ stick cinnamon, and 1 clove garlic (minced or pressed). Cover and cook 5 minutes; stir several times. Stir in 2 teaspoons fine dry bread crumbs and ½ cup grated Parmesan cheese. Remove cinnamon stick; set mixture aside.

(Continued on next page)

Custard Topping. Melt 3 tablespoons butter or margarine in the baking dish; stir in ¼ cup all-purpose flour and cook, uncovered, 1 minute; stir once. Slowly stir in 2 cups milk and cook, uncovered, 4 minutes or until thickened; stir several times. Add ½ teaspoon salt, ⅛ teaspoon ground nutmeg, and ¼ cup grated Parmesan cheese. Slowly beat hot sauce into 3 slightly beaten eggs; set mixture aside.

Corned Beef Brisket with Sour Cream Spinach Soup

The flavorful cooking broth from the corned beef makes a base for spinach soup to serve with the meat. Both can be served hot or cold. Consider using any leftover corned beef in the sandwich recipe that follows. This recipe uses the LOW POWER/DEFROST setting.

    3 pounds corned beef brisket
    1 quart hot water
    1 bay leaf
    1 stick cinnamon (about 3 inches)
    1 small dried hot chile pepper
    ½ teaspoon *each* whole coriander, whole
        allspice, and mustard seed
    1 medium-size onion, sliced
    2 packages (10 or 12 oz. *each*) frozen
        chopped spinach
    2 cups (1 pt.) sour cream

Rinse corned beef well under cold running water. Place in a deep 3½ to 4-quart baking dish. Add hot water, bay leaf, cinnamon stick, chile, coriander, allspice, mustard seed, and onion. Cook, covered, in the microwave oven on the LOW POWER/DEFROST setting for about 2 hours, turning meat over once or twice, until it is tender when pierced.

Remove corned beef from cooking liquid to a carving board. Pour cooking liquid through a wire strainer to remove seasonings. In the baking dish, combine strained broth and spinach. Cook, covered, on REGULAR POWER setting about 10 minutes until spinach is thawed and broth bubbles; break up spinach several times as it softens. Then whirl about a fourth of the mixture at a time in blender to purée. Return puréed mixture to cooking container, smoothly stir in sour cream, and cook, uncovered, 5 minutes until steaming (do not boil); stir several times.

If you wish to serve soup cold, chill it after adding sour cream. Slice brisket and serve warm or cold. Makes 2 quarts soup and brisket for about 6 servings.

Hot Corned Beef and Slaw Sandwiches

Use leftover Corned Beef Brisket (preceding recipe) or purchase sliced cooked corned beef for this hot sandwich with slaw. Homemade or purchased Russian dressing flavors each serving.

    2 tablespoons butter or margarine
    1 small onion, thinly sliced
    3 cups finely shredded green cabbage
    1 teaspoon caraway seed
    2 teaspoons Dijon mustard
    ½ teaspoon garlic salt
    ½ to ¾ pound corned beef, thinly sliced
    4 to 6 large slices rye or dark wheat bread
        Butter
        About 6 ounces Swiss cheese, thinly sliced
    4 to 6 tablespoons Russian dressing

Melt butter in a 7 by 11-inch baking dish, uncovered, in the microwave oven for about 1 minute. Add onion; cover and cook 2 minutes. Stir in shredded cabbage; cover and cook 2 minutes. Add caraway seed, mustard, and garlic salt; stir well to blend. Cover and return to oven.

Place sliced corned beef on a plate, cover, and set plate atop dish of cabbage; cook meat and slaw about 3 minutes or until meat is hot and cabbage limp.

Meanwhile, toast and butter bread. Evenly arrange Swiss cheese slices on toast. Top evenly with hot beef and hot slaw. Spoon about 1 tablespoon Russian dressing over each. Cook, uncovered, about 2 minutes or until cheese begins to melt. Serve with forks and knives. Makes 4 to 6 sandwiches.

Poached Liver

A generous chunk of liver poached in a vegetable-seasoned stock develops a firm texture and succulent flavor distinguishing it from liver that is fried or broiled.

Slice it wafer-thin and serve as a hot entrée. Or chill it in the cooking broth to use like other thinly sliced cold meats.

2 to 2½ pounds unsliced baby beef liver
6 whole black peppers
    About 10 sprigs parsley, broken
1 large onion, cut in wedges
1 large carrot, cut in chunks
1 bay leaf
½ teaspoon salt
1½ to 2 cups water

Place liver, pepper, parsley, onion, carrot, bay, and salt in a deep close-fitting casserole (about 3-quart size—ingredients should nearly fill it). Add water to barely cover liver. Cover casserole and cook in the microwave oven 10 minutes. Remove from oven. Turn liver over in casserole and let stand, covered, for 5 minutes. Then cook, covered, 6 to 10 minutes longer or until meat is no longer pink in center when slashed. Serve hot; or cool in liquid, covered, and then refrigerate until needed (as long as one week). If meat is not completely covered with liquid, turn it over every day or so to keep the whole piece moist. Makes 8 to 10 servings.

Skewered Liver and Bacon

This quick entrée is based on a traditional Swiss dish from Zurich. There, it is accompanied by tiny whole green beans and crusty hashed brown potatoes.

8 slices bacon, cut in halves
    About ½ pound baby beef liver, sliced ¼
        inch thick
    Salt and pepper
¼ teaspoon dried rosemary, crumbled
    Chopped parsley

Arrange bacon on a nonmetallic rack made for microwave ovens or on several thicknesses of paper towels in a 7 by 11-inch baking dish. Cover lightly and cook in the microwave oven 3 to 4 minutes or just until bacon begins to brown. Cool slightly.

Meanwhile, cut liver into 16 equal pieces; sprinkle lightly with salt and pepper, then with rosemary. Wrap each piece in a partially cooked half-slice of bacon, folding liver if necessary. Thread bacon-wrapped liver onto 4 bamboo or wooden skewers, using 4 pieces on each skewer. Place skewers on nonmetallic rack or paper towels in dish. Cook, covered lightly, 3 minutes; turn skewers over, cover, and cook 2 minutes longer or until bacon is crisp and liver is tender but still pink in center. Sprinkle with parsley. Makes 2 servings.

Swiss Sweetbreads

You can cook and prepare the sweetbreads a day ahead; then serve them in a rich, smooth wine-cheese sauce.

1 tablespoon butter or margarine
1½ tablespoons all-purpose flour
    Dash each salt, pepper, and ground
        nutmeg
½ cup regular-strength chicken broth
¼ cup each half-and-half (light cream) and
        dry Vermouth
⅔ cup shredded Swiss cheese
½ teaspoon Dijon mustard
2 pounds cooked sweetbreads (directions
        follow)
    Finely chopped parsley

In a shallow 2-quart baking dish, melt butter in the microwave oven 1 minute until bubbly. Stir in flour, salt, pepper, and nutmeg and cook, uncovered, 1 minute. Gradually stir in broth, cream, and Vermouth. Cook, uncovered, 4 minutes or until thickened; stir often. Stir in cheese and mustard; then add cooked sweetbreads. Cover and cook about 3 minutes or until sweetbreads are hot through; stir several times. Sprinkle with parsley before serving. Makes about 6 servings.

To cook sweetbreads, place 2 pounds sweetbreads in a deep bowl, add water to cover, and soak 1 hour. Drain and place sweetbreads in a 3-quart casserole with ½ cup hot water, 1 tablespoon lemon juice, and 1 teaspoon salt. Cover and cook in the microwave oven 10 to 14 minutes or until sweetbreads are firm and no longer pink throughout. Let stand, covered, about 10 minutes; drain. Remove membrane and tubes with your fingers, separating sweetbreads into small clusters. Reheat in sauce, or cover and refrigerate as long as 24 hours.

*Use full power setting on all recipes
unless otherwise indicated*

Meats   **33**

Veal

Roast Veal with Soubise Sauce

Glistening and golden on the outside, this tender veal roast is succulent and special when sliced. At the table, pass soubise sauce to spoon over the meat.

About 4-pound boned and tied leg of veal
Garlic powder, paprika, and pepper
Water
3 tablespoons butter or margarine
1 cup finely chopped onion
3 tablespoons all-purpose flour
¼ teaspoon ground nutmeg
¾ cup whipping cream
Salt

Lightly rub roast with garlic powder, paprika, and pepper. Place fat side down on a nonmetallic rack made for microwave ovens or on an inverted saucer in a 7 by 11-inch baking dish. Cook, uncovered, in the microwave oven 18 minutes. Turn dish and baste roast often with pan drippings.

Turn roast over, fat side up, and cook, uncovered, about 22 minutes, basting meat and turning dish several times. Remove meat from oven and insert a standard meat thermometer. Let stand, covered, for about 10 minutes to register internal temperature. Thermometer should register 155° to 160°; if not, remove thermometer and return roast to oven for about 5 minutes; then check internal temperature again. When done, lift roast to a warm platter; drain pan drippings into a glass measuring cup and add water, if necessary, to make ¾ cup total. Set aside.

In the dish melt butter 1½ minutes; stir to scrape up browned bits and then stir in onion. Cook, uncovered, 3 to 4 minutes until onion is limp, stirring often. Stir in flour and nutmeg; cook, uncovered, 1 minute or until bubbly. Stir in reserved drippings and cream. Cook, uncovered, 4 to 6 minutes or until thickened and bubbly. Season to taste with salt. Pass in a separate bowl. Makes 8 to 10 servings.

Sherried Veal Kidneys

Veal kidneys, which need only light cooking, adapt well to the microwave oven. Serve them over rice or toasted English muffin halves.

1 pound veal or lamb kidneys (about 5)
Salt and pepper
2 tablespoons butter or margarine
1 tablespoon freeze-dried shallots
1 tablespoon all-purpose flour
1½ teaspoons Dijon mustard
¼ pound fresh mushrooms, sliced
¼ cup dry Sherry
⅓ cup sour cream
Chopped parsley
Hot cooked rice or split and toasted English muffins

Cut away fatty membrane from kidneys and then cut kidneys into ½-inch-thick slices. Sprinkle lightly with salt and pepper. In a shallow 2-quart baking dish, melt butter in the microwave oven 1 minute or until bubbly. Stir in kidneys and shallots. Cover and cook 5 minutes or until kidneys look opaque throughout; stir twice. Remove kidneys from pan.

Stir flour into remaining liquid in baking dish; add mustard, mushrooms, and Sherry, combining well. Cook, uncovered, 3 to 4 minutes or until thickened; stir once or twice.

Return kidneys to baking dish. Smoothly stir in sour cream. Add salt to taste. Cover and cook 2 minutes. Sprinkle with parsley and serve over hot cooked rice or toasted English muffin halves. Makes 4 servings.

Swiss Julienne of Veal

For a bit of table showmanship, turn the hot veal mixture into a chafing dish and flame it in front of your guests.

1 pound boneless veal cutlets, cut about ½ inch thick
Salt, pepper, and paprika
3 tablespoons butter or margarine
2 tablespoons chopped green onion or shallots
¼ pound mushrooms, sliced
2 tablespoons all-purpose flour
¼ cup dry white wine
½ cup whipping cream
2 tablespoons brandy

Carefully trim away membrane from veal. Place one piece at a time between two pieces of wax paper and pound with a smooth-surfaced mallet to flatten it evenly to about ¼-inch thickness. Sprinkle meat lightly on each side with salt, pepper, and paprika. Cut into strips ¼ inch wide and about 1½ inches long.

In a 7 by 11-inch baking dish, melt 2 tablespoons of the butter in the microwave oven 1½ minutes. Stir in green onion and mushrooms. Cook, uncovered, 3 minutes, stirring once. Add veal strips and cook, uncovered, 5 minutes or until no longer pink throughout; stir several times. Lift meat and vegetables from drippings and set aside. Pour juices into a glass measuring cup (you should have about ½ cup liquid).

Melt remaining tablespoon butter in baking dish 1½ minutes. Stir in flour and cook, uncovered, 1 minute. Stir in veal juices, wine, and cream. Cook, uncovered, 3 minutes, until smooth and thickened; stir twice. (At this point, the sauce and meat can be refrigerated separately if made ahead.)

To serve, add meat to hot sauce (if refrigerated, reheat sauce, uncovered, until bubbly; then add meat) and cook, uncovered, 2 minutes or until hot through. Put brandy in a small ceramic container; heat, uncovered, 10 seconds or until warm to touch. Ignite brandy, pour over meat in sauce, stir until flames die down, and then serve. Makes 4 servings.

Chinese Steamed Flower Buns

Because these snowy white buns are traditionally steamed, they adapt beautifully to microwave cooking. The Chinese serve them with roast meat or duck. Try them with the baked ham recipe on page 38.

This recipe uses purchased frozen bread dough to make the flower rolls.

To thaw frozen bread dough, lightly brush frozen dough with salad oil and place in a glass 5 by 9-inch loaf pan. *If you have a defrost cycle on your microwave oven,* defrost 2 minutes, turning loaf over every 30 seconds (giving pan quarter turns). If your oven doesn't have a defrost cycle, *cook on regular cycle* 1 minute, turning loaf over every 15 seconds (giving pan quarter turns). In either case, don't overheat dough, as yeast may be destroyed.

Divide thawed loaf into 16 equal pieces; shape each into a ball and then roll into a 3-inch round and brush surface with salad oil. Fold circles in half and place four or five buns in 9-inch pie plates or 9-inch square baking dish. Cover loosely and let dough rise about 30 minutes or until doubled in size. (Place rolls in the refrigerator if you don't want to cook them all at one time.)

Cook one plate of rolls at a time, uncovered, in the microwave oven 1 minute. Remove from plate and turn upside-down to dry bottom sides of buns. Serve with sliced meats or alone. Makes 16 steamed buns.

Pork

Soy-honey Sauce for Sausages

When you use fully cooked sausages you've already saved one preparation step. Good choices for this recipe are Polish sausage (kielbasa), knackwurst (garlic frankfurters), smoked sausage links, bratwurst, frankfurters, or cooked pork sausage links.

- **1 to 1½ pounds fully cooked sausages (see suggestions above)**
- **¼ cup *each* honey and soy sauce**
- **3 tablespoons chile sauce or catsup**
- **1 tablespoon vinegar**
- **¼ teaspoon garlic powder**

Cut ¼-inch-deep slashes in sausages at about 1-inch intervals. Place in an 8-inch-square baking dish. Cook, covered, in the microwave oven 4 minutes, turning sausages over once or twice; drain off any fat.

In a glass measuring cup, combine honey, soy sauce, chile sauce, vinegar, and garlic powder. Cook, uncovered, 3 minutes or until sauce is clear and thickened. Serve over sausages. Makes 4 servings.

Polish Sausage with Cabbage

Spicy sausages lend their pleasing seasonings to the cabbage in this meal-in-one-dish.

- **2 tablespoons butter or margarine**
- **2 green onions, thinly sliced (including part of tops)**
- **1 small head cabbage (about 1¼ lb.)**
- **½ teaspoon salt**
- **Dash pepper**
- **1 pound Polish sausage (kielbasa)**

In a 7 by 11-inch baking dish, melt butter 1½ minutes in the microwave oven. Add green onions and cook, uncovered, 1½ minutes. Core and coarsely shred cabbage. Stir into onion mixture. Add salt and pepper.

Cut ¼-inch-deep slashes in sausages at about 1-inch intervals. Remove metal end fasteners, if any. Place atop cabbage. Cover and cook 12 to 14 minutes, turning sausages over once or twice. Makes 4 servings.

Prune-glazed Oven Pork Stew

Pork butt is usually a good buy for family meals and it doesn't require long cooking to become juicy and tender. Onions and prunes join the cubed meat in a spicy sauce for a quick stew.

1¼ to 1½ pounds lean pork butt, boned
½ cup prune juice
1½ teaspoons lemon juice
½ teaspoon salt
¼ teaspoon dried rosemary, crushed
⅛ teaspoon *each* ground cinnamon, ginger, and pepper
1 tablespoon cornstarch mixed with 1 tablespoon water
1 can (1 lb.) small boiling onions, drained
16 pitted prunes

Cut meat into 1-inch cubes; place in a 7 by 11-inch baking dish. Cook pork, covered, in the microwave oven 10 minutes, stirring once or twice to reposition pieces from middle to outside edges. Drain off liquid into a 4-cup glass measure and set meat aside, covered.

Skim and discard fat from meat juices; then mix in prune juice, lemon juice, salt, rosemary, cinnamon, ginger, pepper, and cornstarch mixed with water. Cook, uncovered, 3 minutes or until bubbling, thickened, and clear. Add sauce to meat and stir in onions and prunes. Cook, uncovered, about 1 minute to heat through. Serves 4.

Lemony Country-style Ribs

Meaty country-style ribs cook slowly on the LOW POWER/DEFROST setting of the microwave oven. Ribs are flavored with lemon and ginger.

1 large onion, finely chopped
1 lemon, thinly sliced
3 pounds country-style spareribs
⅓ cup honey
½ cup soy sauce
¼ cup lemon juice
1 teaspoon grated fresh ginger
1 clove garlic, minced or pressed
1 tablespoon *each* cornstarch and water

Arrange onion and lemon in a 10-inch-square covered baking dish; top with spareribs. Cover and cook in the microwave oven on REGULAR POWER setting 10 minutes. Meanwhile, combine honey, soy, lemon juice, ginger, and garlic. Pour honey mixture over partially cooked spareribs. Cover and cook on LOW POWER/DEFROST setting 45 minutes to 1 hour, turning once, until spareribs are tender. Lift out spareribs and skim off and discard fat from drippings. Combine cornstarch with water; add to drippings. Cook, uncovered, on REGULAR POWER setting 4 to 5 minutes or until thickened, stirring once or twice. Return ribs to sauce, reheating if necessary, and serve. Makes 4 servings.

Hot Dogs— a Household Institution

In just 45 seconds your microwave oven turns out a frankfurter cooked in a bun. If both meat and bun are frozen, simply double the cooking time.

For franks *con queso*, make a lengthwise slit in each frankfurter, being careful not to cut through. Place a thin piece of jack cheese and a strip of canned California green chile in the slit. Spread taco sauce or mustard on the frankfurter bun. Place frank in bun. Wrap bun in a paper towel or napkin. Heat 45 seconds. Add 45 seconds more for each additional frankfurter placed in the oven at the same time.

Oven-fried Pork Chops with Mushrooms

Well-seasoned crumbs give a crisp coating to these tender, juicy chops served with a green onion-mushroom sauce.

  6 tablespoons butter or margarine
  ½ pound mushrooms, sliced
  1 clove garlic, minced or pressed
  ¼ teaspoon dried rosemary, crumbled
  ½ cup whipping cream
  ¼ cup thinly sliced green onions
      Salt and pepper
  2 tablespoons *each* grated Parmesan cheese
      and cornmeal
  3 tablespoons fine dry bread crumbs
  ½ teaspoon *each* garlic salt and oregano
      leaves
  4 lean pork chops, cut ½ inch thick

In a 7 by 11-inch baking dish heat 2 tablespoons of the butter 30 seconds in the microwave oven. Add mushrooms and garlic and cook, uncovered, 2 minutes, stirring once. Stir in rosemary and cream and cook, uncovered, 5 minutes or until sauce is bubbling and reduced to about ¼ cup. Stir in green onions and season to taste with salt and pepper. Turn into a small serving bowl and set aside. Wash dish.

In a bag, combine cheese, cornmeal, bread crumbs, garlic salt, and oregano. Melt remaining butter in baking dish 1 minute. Dip each chop into butter, drain briefly, then shake each in crumb mixture. Shake off excess coating and arrange chops in baking dish or on a nonmetallic rack in dish, placing meatiest portions toward edges of dish. Cook pork chops, uncovered, 5 minutes. Turn meat over and cook, uncovered, 5 minutes or until meat shows no pink color in thickest portions when slashed.

Pass bowl of mushroom sauce at table (reheat briefly if needed). Makes 4 servings.

Pork Loin with Plum Sauce

Prepare plum sauce as directed on page 43 for Roast Chicken with Plum Sauce. Cover and refrigerate half the sauce to use another time on chicken or pork. It keeps well for 3 to 4 weeks.

  3½ to 4-pound boned and tied pork loin
        About 1 cup plum sauce (see page 43)

Place roast, fat side down, on an inverted saucer or nonmetallic rack made for microwave ovens, in a 7 by 11-inch baking dish. Cook, uncovered, in the microwave oven 10 minutes, turning dish several times. Generously spoon plum sauce over meat and cook, uncovered, 10 minutes, turning dish several times.

Turn roast fat side up and cook, uncovered, 10 minutes, turning dish several times. Baste generously with sauce and cook, uncovered, 10 more minutes or until a meat thermometer inserted in center of meat registers 160°. Remove roast to a serving platter and let stand, covered, 5 to 10 minutes until meat thermometer registers 170°.

Skim and discard fat from pan drippings; stir drippings into any remaining plum sauce. Cook sauce, uncovered, 1 minute or until hot. Pass in a separate bowl. Makes 6 to 8 servings.

Chile Frank Enchiladas

You can use regular or garlic frankfurters or smoked sausage links to stuff these enchiladas. Spoon canned chile over franks, roll in a tortilla, top with sauce, and bake.

  1 tablespoon salad oil
  1 small onion, chopped
  2 tablespoons seeded and chopped canned
      California green chiles
  1 can (8 oz.) tomato sauce
  4 drops liquid hot pepper seasoning
  6 corn tortillas
  6 frankfurters
  1 can (15 oz.) chile (with or without beans)
  1½ cups shredded Cheddar or jack cheese

Pour oil into a 9-inch pie plate. Add onion and cook, uncovered, in the microwave oven 5 minutes or until limp; stir once. Stir in chiles, tomato sauce, and hot pepper seasoning; heat, uncovered, 3 minutes until sauce is bubbling around edges.

Dip each tortilla into sauce; drain briefly. Place a frankfurter on top and spoon over about 1/6 of the chile; then sprinkle with about 1½ tablespoons of the cheese. Roll tortilla and place, seam side down, in a 7 by 11-inch baking dish; repeat with remaining ingredients. Pour remaining sauce over top.

Cover and cook 5 minutes, turning dish once. Sprinkle with remaining cheese; cook, uncovered, 5 minutes or until heated through and cheese is melted. Makes 6 enchiladas.

Oven-barbecue Spareribs

Have plenty of napkins handy—you'll want to pick up these spareribs seasoned with lemon slices and spicy tomato sauce.

    1 side spareribs (about 3 lb.) snipped apart
        between bones
    2 tablespoons lemon juice
 2½ tablespoons chile sauce or catsup
    ½ teaspoon prepared horseradish
 1½ teaspoons Worcestershire
    ¼ teaspoon *each* salt and paprika
    ¼ cup orange juice
    1 teaspoon dry mustard
    2 tablespoons firmly packed brown sugar
    1 small clove garlic, minced or pressed
    1 lemon, sliced

Arrange spareribs in a 7 by 11-inch baking dish with large ends toward the edges of dish and meatiest sides down. Cover lightly with paper towels and cook in the microwave oven 7 minutes, turning ribs over once; drain off and discard fat.

Meanwhile, mix together lemon juice, chile sauce, horseradish, Worcestershire, salt, paprika, orange juice, mustard, brown sugar, and garlic. Pour over ribs. Cook, lightly covered, 20 minutes, turning ribs and repositioning them in the dish every 5 minutes. Serve with lemon wedges tucked between ribs. Makes 2 servings.

Baked Ham with Spicy Orange Glaze

This simple, stir-together glaze contributes sophisticated flavor to canned ham—and the ham is ready to serve in less than 15 minutes.

    ⅓ cup orange marmalade
 1½ tablespoons Dijon mustard
    ⅛ teaspoon ground cloves
    1 can (1½ lb.) fully cooked ham

Stir together marmalade, mustard, and cloves. Remove ham from can and place in a 7 by 11-inch baking dish; spoon or brush about half the marmalade mixture evenly over top and sides. Cover lightly and cook in the microwave oven about 4 minutes. Turn ham over, brush with more marmalade mixture, and cook, uncovered, 5 minutes or until heated through. Let stand, covered, 5 minutes. Stir any remaining glaze into pan drippings; pass at the table to spoon over individual slices. Makes 4 to 6 servings.

For canned hams weighing more than 1½ pounds but less than 5 pounds, double the glaze recipe and allow 6 minutes cooking time per pound; for those over 5 pounds, triple the glaze recipe and allow 7 minutes cooking time per pound.

Lamb

Fruited Lamb Stew

Dried fruits become juicy when cooked with the vegetables in a lamb stew. This recipe uses the LOW POWER/DEFROST setting.

 1½ pounds boneless lamb stew meat cut into
        1-inch cubes
    Salt and pepper
    ½ teaspoon ground ginger
    2 cloves garlic, minced or pressed
    1 stick cinnamon, 2 to 3 inches long, broken
        into thirds
    1 small can (12 oz.) cocktail vegetable juice
    3 large carrots, cut in 1-inch slices
    1 small eggplant (about 1 lb.), cut into 1½-
        inch cubes
    1 package (6 oz.) dried apricots or pitted
        prunes
    1 tablespoon *each* cornstarch and water

Place lamb in a 10-inch-square covered baking dish. Sprinkle lightly with salt and pepper; then mix in ginger and garlic, add cinnamon stick, and pour on vegetable juice. Cover and cook in the microwave oven at LOW POWER/DEFROST setting 20 minutes. Stir in carrots, eggplant, and apricots; then cover and continue to cook on REGULAR POWER setting 15 minutes or until meat and vegetables are tender when pierced. Meanwhile, blend cornstarch and water in a 4-cup glass measure.

Drain liquid from lamb into cornstarch mixture. Cook on REGULAR POWER setting 2 to 3 minutes until thickened and clear, stirring once or twice. Pour over lamb. Makes about 4 servings.

Grilled Lamb Patties

The bite of curry in these patties is tempered by a sauce of chutney and unflavored yogurt.

38 Meats

1 pound lean ground lamb
1 teaspoon instant minced onion
¼ cup fine dry bread crumbs
1 egg
⅓ cup raisins
½ teaspoon *each* garlic salt and curry powder
¼ teaspoon ground cinnamon
⅛ teaspoon *each* ground nutmeg and pepper
   Unflavored yogurt
   Major Grey's chutney, finely chopped

Combine lamb, onion, bread crumbs, egg, raisins, garlic salt, curry powder, cinnamon, nutmeg, and pepper. Divide mixture into 4 equal portions; shape each into a patty ½ to ¾ inch thick.

Place patties on a nonmetallic rack made for microwave ovens, in a 7 by 11-inch baking dish (or place patties directly in baking dish). Cook, covered lightly, in the microwave oven 6 minutes or until meat is no longer pink when slashed; turn patties over and reposition them on rack once or twice. Serve with a bowl of unflavored yogurt seasoned to taste with finely chopped Major Grey's chutney. Makes 4 servings.

Marinated Lamb Chops, Portuguese-style

An overnight soaking in a cumin-cinnamon flavored wine marinade tenderizes and seasons shoulder lamb chops.

½ cup dry red wine
2 tablespoons olive oil or salad oil
2 small cloves garlic, minced or pressed
½ teaspoon salt
1 teaspoon ground cumin
½ teaspoon ground cinnamon
2½ tablespoons instant minced onion
4 shoulder lamp chops (about 1¾ lb.) *each* cut about ¾ inch thick

In a 7 by 11-inch baking dish, combine wine, oil, garlic, salt, cumin, cinnamon, and onion. Stir well. Place lamb chops in marinade, turning to moisten all sides, and arrange in a single layer. Cover and refrigerate at least 8 hours or overnight. Turn chops over in marinade occasionally.

Drain off marinade (reserve for other uses) and cook lamb chops, uncovered, in the microwave oven 3 minutes. Turn chops over and reposition them in the dish. Cook, uncovered, 3 minutes for medium (add 1 additional minute for well-done). Let stand, covered, 5 to 7 minutes before serving. Makes 4 servings.

Lamb, Persian-style

Fresh peaches or nectarines accompany spicy lamb chunks. Unflavored yogurt as a sauce gives an extra touch of the Middle East. This recipe uses the LOW POWER/DEFROST setting.

2 pounds lean boneless lamb shoulder, cut in bite-size pieces
½ teaspoon salt
¼ teaspoon pepper
1 teaspoon *each* ground cinnamon and cloves
2 tablespoons firmly packed brown sugar
1 medium-size onion, chopped
2 tablespoons lemon juice
2 teaspoons cornstarch
1 tablespoon water
   About 1 pound nectarines or peaches
1½ tablespoons butter or margarine
   Unflavored yogurt

Arrange lamb in a shallow 2-quart baking dish. Mix together salt, pepper, cinnamon, cloves, and brown sugar; sprinkle over lamb. Top with onion and lemon juice. Cover and cook in the microwave oven at LOW POWER/DEFROST setting 30 to 35 minutes until lamb is tender when pierced, stirring once or twice.

In a 2-cup glass measure, mix cornstarch and water. Drain liquid from lamb mixture into cornstarch. Cook, uncovered, on REGULAR POWER setting 2 to 3 minutes until thickened. Pour sauce over lamb.

Pit nectarines or peeled peaches and cut into thick slices. Melt butter 1 minute in a 9-inch pie plate; stir in fruit and cook, uncovered, on REGULAR POWER setting about 1½ minutes (just until heated through). Arrange on top of the meat. Serve with unflavored yogurt. Makes 4 servings.

Poultry

How to cook the big birds...and the small ones

Cooked by microwaves, poultry becomes tender in a matter of minutes—and the meat will be extremely juicy. But because poultry pieces (and even whole birds) cook so fast, they brown less than when cooked in a conventional oven.

Lack of browning is no problem when you simply want cooked meat for sandwiches or cooked chicken pieces for use in casseroles. But when eye appeal counts, there are some easy ways to overcome the pale appearance:

• Brown the microwave-cooked bird (except turkey) 3 or 4 inches below a preheated broiler before serving, watching it carefully until the skin is crisp and browned.

• Partially cook chicken and turkey pieces in the microwave oven and finish them on the barbecue.

• Liberally baste the skin with a sauce, adding distinctive flavor along with rich color.

For attractive oven-fried chicken, you can shake the pieces in crumb mixtures and then sprinkle with paprika before cooking.

Cook whole birds breast side down for the first half of the cooking time, then breast side up until done. You'll need to elevate the bird above the pan juices on a nonmetallic rack made for microwave ovens (available in some appliance stores) or on an inverted saucer.

Cook cut-up poultry in a shallow dish wide enough to cook pieces in a single layer for even heat penetration; arrange meatiest portions near edges of dish with drumstick ends, wings, and backs in center.

Cook all poultry just until it loses its pinkness when slashed near the bone; then cover and let stand briefly before serving. Meat will continue to cook a few minutes. Total cooking time is about the same whether the bird is roasted stuffed or unstuffed.

Giblet lovers should stick to conventional cooking. In the microwave, the gizzard and heart tend to become tough, and whole livers may explode.

Roasted Whole Birds

Chicken, turkey, duckling, and Rock Cornish game hens can be roasted using the same general procedure. (Also see additional information under individual kind of bird.)

To prepare a whole bird for roasting, remove giblets and save to cook conventionally. Rinse bird and pat dry, inside and out. Salt poultry after cooking so meat retains maximum moisture. Loosely stuff the bird, if you wish. Close the neck and body cavities by fastening them with wooden picks or sewing them with string. Secure wings akimbo style (tucking wings under the back of the bird).

Place bird, breast side down, on a nonmetallic rack made for microwave ovens or on an inverted saucer in a shallow baking dish and cook, uncovered, for half the estimated time (see chart that follows). Turn dish around in oven several times for more even cooking. As drippings accumulate, pour off and reserve for basting and gravy, if desired.

When bird is half cooked, turn it, breast up, and continue cooking on the rack for the remainder of the estimated time. Baste with drippings and turn dish several times. Remove from oven and let stand, covered, 5 to 10 minutes before serving.

Turkey. Select a turkey that will comfortably fit in your baking dish with nonmetallic rack and also fit in the oven. It is often more practical and easier to cook large turkeys conventionally. Cook for the estimated time. Remove from oven and insert a meat thermometer in thickest part of thigh. When done, it should reach 180° to 185° after a 10-minute standing period. The drumstick should move easily when jiggled, and thigh meat should feel soft when pinched.

Chicken. Cook for the estimated time; let stand 5 to 10 minutes. Test large chickens for doneness with a meat thermometer as for turkey. Smaller birds are done when the drumstick moves easily when jiggled or when meat near thigh bone is no longer pink when slashed. For a crisp, brown skin, place chicken, breast side down, on a heatproof platter 3 to 4 inches below a preheated broiler. Watch carefully until browned to your liking; turn breast side up and cook until browned.

Rock Cornish Game Hens. Cook only the number of birds at one time that will comfortably fit your baking dish with its rack and fit the oven so the microwaves can readily penetrate all surfaces. If you're cooking more than one, base the estimated cooking time on the hens' collective weight. When done, the legs should move freely and meat should no longer be pink near bone when slashed. Skin may be browned under the broiler.

Wild Duck and Domestic Duckling. Before cooking, generously prick skin with the tines of a fork to allow fat just under the skin to drain into the dish during cooking. Then frequently pour drippings out of baking dish to cut down on oven splatter. Cook for the estimated time; duck is done when drumstick moves easily when jiggled. Skin may be browned under the broiler.

Baked Chicken Breasts

By using your microwave oven, you can have cooked chicken breast meat on hand in minutes.

Use 2 whole chicken breasts (about 1½ lb.), cut in halves. Place them in a 7 by 11-inch baking dish and cook, covered, 5 to 7 minutes or until meat is no longer pink in thickest portion when slashed with a knife. Turn chicken over several times. Let stand 5 to 10 minutes; then remove and discard skin and bones. Pour off liquid and save as chicken broth to use in other recipes. Cut chicken in pieces as called for in the recipe you're using. Makes about 2 cups cubed chicken.

Poultry Cooking Times

Either stuffed or unstuffed, whole birds take about the same amount of time to cook. Cooking time for cut-up birds depends on the pieces you select.

Whole Birds (Cooking Time Per Pound)

Turkey	7 to 8 minutes
Chicken	6 to 7 minutes
Rock Cornish Game Hens	About 6 minutes
Wild Duck	About 5 minutes
Domestic Duckling	About 8 minutes

Poultry Pieces

Turkey breast	About 4 minutes
Whole broiler-fryer, cut-up	6 to 7 minutes
Chicken breast	About 4 minutes
Chicken legs (thighs attached)	About 7 minutes

Baked Turkey Breast

When you need 6 to 7 cups of cooked poultry for a company-size entrée, such as a main-dish salad, casserole, or curry dish, you can quickly bake half a turkey breast in your microwave oven while you assemble the other ingredients.

Select a half turkey breast weighing about 3½ pounds. If the breast is frozen, thaw at room temperature or in your microwave oven according to manufacturer's directions.

Place breast, skin side down, in a 7 by 11-inch baking dish. Cover and cook in the microwave oven 6 minutes, turning dish 2 or 3 times. Turn breast, skin side up, and cook, covered, 8 to 10 minutes longer or until meat is no longer pink when slashed in thickest portion. Let stand, covered, about 5 minutes. When cool enough to handle, discard skin and bones; cut meat into bite-size pieces. Save drippings from baking dish to use for broth. Makes 6 to 7 cups cooked meat and about 1 cup broth.

Roast Chicken with Plum Sauce

Based on one can of purple plums, this recipe makes enough sauce for two meals. Covered and refrigerated, the sauce keeps well 3 to 4 weeks.

- 1 can (1 lb.) whole purple plums
- 2 tablespoons butter or margarine
- 1 medium-size onion, chopped
- ¼ cup firmly packed brown sugar
- ¼ cup tomato-based chile sauce
- 2 tablespoons soy sauce
- 1 teaspoon ground ginger
- 2 teaspoons lemon juice
- 3 to 3½-pound whole broiler-fryer chicken
  Pepper

Drain plums, saving 2 tablespoons of the syrup. Remove pits; then whirl plums and reserved syrup in a blender until puréed. Set aside.

Melt butter in a 7 by 11-inch baking dish in the microwave oven; add onion and cook, uncovered, for 2 minutes. Stir in sugar, chile sauce, soy sauce, ginger, lemon juice, and the plum purée. Cook, uncovered, stirring several times, for 5 minutes or until sauce is slightly thickened. Pour into a 2-cup glass measure and set aside; wipe out baking dish.

Reserve giblets and neck for other uses. Rinse chicken and pat dry; sprinkle cavities and skin with salt and pepper. Secure wings akimbo style, fasten skin across neck opening to back with a wooden pick, and tie drumsticks together. Place chicken breast side down in the baking dish on a nonmetallic rack or inverted saucer. Cook, uncovered, for 6 minutes. Brush generously with plum sauce, and cook 6 minutes longer.

Remove from oven, turn chicken breast side up, and cook, uncovered, for 6 minutes. Brush generously with plum sauce and cook 6 minutes longer or until thigh meat is no longer pink near bone when slashed. Transfer chicken to a warm serving platter; remove string and pick; keep chicken warm. Drain juices from baking dish into a glass measure; skim and discard fat. Stir in about ⅓ cup plum sauce and cook, uncovered, for about 1 minute or until heated through. Pass sauce in a separate bowl.

Cover and refrigerate leftover plum sauce to use on another chicken or pork roast (see page 37). Makes about 4 servings.

Swiss Chicken

Boned chicken breasts, masked with a creamy smooth wine-flavored cheese sauce, are an easy but elegant entrée for two.

- 1 large whole chicken breast, split (about 1 lb.)
- ¼ teaspoon paprika
- 1 teaspoon cornstarch
- 2 tablespoons dry Sherry or apple juice
- ⅓ cup half-and-half (light cream)
- ½ cup shredded Swiss cheese
  Chopped parsley

Skin and bone chicken breasts; place flat side down in a shallow baking dish. Combine paprika and cornstarch; stir in Sherry and cream and pour over chicken. Cover and cook in the microwave oven 1 minute; stir sauce and cook, covered, for 2 more minutes. Stir sauce well, sprinkle cheese over chicken and cook, uncovered, about 1½ minutes or until cheese melts and meat is no longer pink when slashed. Spoon sauce over chicken; garnish with parsley. Makes 2 servings.

Which Came First? For Breakfast, the Egg

Just seconds make a difference between a perfectly cooked egg and one that's overcooked in the microwave oven. Since eggs cook with lightning speed, careful watching is a must.

If you've ever fried an egg over a conventional burner, you've probably noticed the white becomes firm first. That's because it coagulates at a lower temperature than the yolk. But in the microwave oven, the egg yolk, having a higher fat content than the white, attracts more microwave energy and cooks first. Adding other ingredients to the egg dish (even water for poaching) or scrambling the eggs to mix up the yolks makes for more even cooking.

We found eggs are at their best when poached, baked, or scrambled. For testing, we used regular large eggs.

Do not soft-cook or hard-cook eggs in their shells in the microwave oven. They might explode from the pressure that builds up inside the shell with such rapid cooking.

Poached Eggs

Four-inch custard cups are perfect containers for poaching eggs—the eggs emerge plump and round, ready to enjoy.

For 1 egg, heat ¼ cup hot tap water and ¼ teaspoon white vinegar to boiling in a 4-inch custard cup (or 4 to 5-inch-diameter bowl) in the microwave oven (takes about 30 seconds). Break 1 egg into the water, cover tightly, and cook 30 seconds or just until yolk films over. Let stand, covered, 1 minute. To serve, lift egg from water with slotted spoon.

For more than 1 egg, add 30 seconds more cooking time for each additional egg in individual container (2 eggs, 1 minute).

Baked Eggs in Hash

Divide 1 can (12 oz.) corned beef hash evenly between 2 custard cups (each about 4 inches in diameter). With the back of a spoon, make a hollow in the center of the hash. Break 1 egg into each indentation. Sprinkle each egg with 1 tablespoon shredded Cheddar cheese. Cook, covered, in the microwave oven 4½ minutes or until hash is hot and egg white is nearly opaque. Let stand, covered, 1 minute. Makes 2 servings.

Shirred Eggs

In conventional cooking, "shirring" usually refers to baking eggs with meat, cheese, or other savory ingredients. Here, shirred eggs make great time-saving one-dish breakfasts from the microwave.

Cheese and Onion Egg. In a 4-inch custard cup, melt 1 teaspoon butter or margarine 30 seconds in the microwave oven. Add 1 green onion, sliced, and cook, uncovered, 1½ minutes until tender. Break 1 egg into the cup and sprinkle with 1 tablespoon shredded Cheddar cheese. Cover and cook 30 seconds until egg is almost set. Let stand, covered, 1 minute. Sprinkle lightly with salt and pepper to taste. Makes 1 serving.

Sausages and Egg. Place 2 brown-and-serve pork sausage links in a 4-inch custard cup. Cover with paper towel and cook in the microwave oven 30 seconds. Pour off any drippings. Break 1 egg into cup between the sausages and top with 1 tablespoon grated Parmesan cheese. Cover and cook 1 minute or until egg is almost set. Let stand, covered, 1 minute. Makes 1 serving.

Ham, Egg, and Cheese. Place a thin, 4½-inch-square slice of cooked ham snugly into a 4-inch custard cup. Cover with paper towel and cook in the microwave oven 1 minute until edges begin to brown. Break 1 egg onto the ham and sprinkle with 1 tablespoon shredded jack, Samsoe, Swiss, or fontina cheese. Cover and cook 35 seconds until egg is almost set. Let stand, covered, 1 minute. Makes 1 serving.

Creamy Scrambled Eggs

In a small glass bowl or measuring cup, melt 2 teaspoons butter or margarine in the microwave oven 30 seconds. Stir in 2 teaspoons all-purpose flour. Cook, uncovered, 30 seconds until bubbly. Blend in ⅓ cup sour cream and cook, uncovered, 1 minute until bubbly and smooth, stirring once. Set aside.

In a 10-inch glass pie plate, melt 1 tablespoon butter or margarine 30 seconds. Lightly beat together 8 eggs with ¼ teaspoon salt and ⅛ teaspoon pepper. Pour into pie plate and cook, uncovered, 3 to 4 minutes (or until just set to your liking), stirring often with a fork to push cooked portions toward center of dish. Remove from oven and fold in sour cream mixture. Garnish with minced parsley or thinly sliced green onion. Makes 4 servings.

Chicken Teriyaki with Vegetables

Garden vegetables and a plump bird, cooked in sequence, make up the decorative dish shown on our cover. The chicken can be stuffed with a packaged rice mix, if you like.

    1 teaspoon sesame seed
    1 package (6 oz.) chicken-flavored rice mix
      (optional)
      About ¾ pound broccoli
    8 small whole carrots
    2 tablespoons water
      About 3½-pound whole broiler-fryer chicken
    ⅓ cup soy sauce
    2 tablespoons *each* sugar and dry Sherry
    ¼ teaspoon ground ginger
    2 cloves garlic, minced or pressed
    1½ teaspoons cornstarch
    1 can (1 lb.) small whole onions, drained
    2 tablespoons melted butter or margarine

Place sesame seed in a 7 by 11-inch baking dish. Cook, uncovered, in the microwave oven about 2½ minutes or until golden, stirring often; set seed aside.

Prepare rice mix according to package directions if you choose to stuff the chicken; set aside.

Trim and discard tough broccoli stems; cut spears into 2 or 3 thin lengthwise pieces; set aside. Place carrots in a 7 by 11-inch baking dish; drizzle with water, cover, and cook 5 minutes or until just tender when pierced (turn dish several times). Lift out carrots, add broccoli, cover, and cook 3½ minutes or until just tender when pierced. Lift out broccoli and drain liquid from dish into a glass measure; set aside.

Reserve chicken giblets and neck for other uses. Rinse chicken and pat dry; stuff body cavity with cooked rice, if desired (save any that is left to pass at the table), and close opening with a wooden pick. Secure wings akimbo style, fasten neck skin under wings if possible, and tie drumsticks together. Place chicken, breast side down, in the baking dish on an inverted saucer or nonmetallic rack; cook, uncovered, for 6 minutes. Remove from oven.

Meanwhile, stir soy, sugar, Sherry, ginger, garlic, and cornstarch into vegetable liquid in glass measure; cook, uncovered, for 1 to 1½ minutes or until bubbly and clear, stirring frequently. Brush sauce over chicken and cook, uncovered, 6 minutes longer. Turn chicken breast up and cook, uncovered, for 6 minutes; brush generously with sauce and cook 6 minutes longer or until thigh meat is no longer pink near bone when slashed. Arrange carrots, broccoli, and onions around chicken; brush vegetables with melted butter, sprinkle carrots with sesame seed, and cook, uncovered, 1 to 2 minutes longer or until vegetables are heated through. Reheat remaining teriyaki sauce about 1 minute and pass at the table (also reheat any remaining rice mix, if used). Makes 4 servings.

Oven-fried Chicken Parmesan

If you like to eat chicken with your fingers, you'll appreciate these well-seasoned, crumb-coated pieces. Try one of the two variations that follow.

In a bag, combine 1 tablespoon *each* grated Parmesan cheese and cornmeal, 1½ tablespoons fine dry bread crumbs, and ¼ teaspoon *each* garlic salt and oregano leaves. Melt 2 tablespoons butter or margarine in a shallow baking dish in microwave oven 1 minute. Rinse 2 chicken legs with thighs attached; pat dry. Turn chicken pieces over in the butter, drain briefly, and shake in the crumb mixture to coat evenly. Arrange in the baking dish (or on a nonmetallic rack in the baking dish) with thighs toward edge of dish and ends of drumsticks in the center; sprinkle top with paprika. Cook, uncovered, for 5 minutes; turn pan and cook for 2 minutes more or until thigh meat is no longer pink near bone when slashed. Let stand about 5 minutes before serving. Serves 2.

Paprika-fried Chicken. Follow the directions for preparing and cooking Oven-fried Chicken Parmesan but substitute this flour mixture for the cheese-cornmeal mixture. Combine 3 tablespoons all-purpose flour, 1 teaspoon *each* paprika and poultry seasoning, ½ teaspoon salt, and ¼ teaspoon garlic powder.

Stuffing-coated Chicken. Follow the directions for preparing and cooking Oven-fried Chicken Parmesan but substitute about ⅓ cup finely crushed packaged stuffing mix or herb-seasoned croutons for the cheese-cornmeal mixture.

Grecian Chicken with Artichokes

Artichoke hearts and toasted nuts elevate this chicken casserole to company status. It's ready to eat in about 30 minutes.

  ¼ cup pine nuts or slivered almonds
  2 cups quick-cooking brown rice
  1 package (9 oz.) frozen artichoke hearts, thawed
  1 cup regular-strength chicken broth
  ¼ cup dry white wine
  2 tablespoons instant minced onion
  1 teaspoon salt
  ½ teaspoon grated lemon peel
  ½ teaspoon oregano leaves
    3-pound broiler-fryer chicken, cut up
    Paprika

Spread pine nuts or almonds in a shallow baking dish (about 7 by 11 inches) and cook, uncovered, in the microwave oven until lightly browned, 2 to 3 minutes. Turn out of dish and set aside.

In the same dish combine rice, artichokes, broth, wine, onion, salt, lemon peel, and oregano. Arrange chicken pieces, skin side up, in a single layer over the rice mixture, with meatiest pieces toward edge of dish. Sprinkle lightly with paprika. Cover and cook 18 to 22 minutes, giving dish quarter turns every 5 minutes, until meat is no longer pink near bone when slashed. Let stand, covered, for about 5 minutes. Sprinkle with toasted nuts. Makes about 4 servings.

Chicken Saltimbocca

This version of the popular Italian entrée uses boned and pounded chicken breasts instead of the traditional thin-sliced veal.

  1 whole chicken breast (about 1 lb.), halved, boned, and skinned
  2 slices (about 1 oz. *each*) jack cheese
  2 slices (about 1 oz. *each*) boiled ham
  2 tablespoons butter or margarine
    Salt, pepper, and ground nutmeg
  4 to 6 large mushrooms, sliced
  2 tablespoons cream Sherry or Marsala
    Chopped parsley

Place each piece of chicken on a piece of waxed paper; cover with another piece of waxed paper and pound meat firmly with a flat mallet until about ¼ inch thick. Place 1 slice cheese and 1 slice ham on each chicken piece; then fold each chicken piece in half to enclose cheese and ham; secure with a wooden pick.

Melt butter in a shallow baking dish in the microwave oven 1 minute; turn chicken bundles over in butter to coat all sides. Lift out and sprinkle lightly with salt, pepper, and nutmeg. Add mushrooms to dish and cook, uncovered, for 1 to 1½ minutes. Stir mushrooms, arrange chicken over top, cover, and cook 4 minutes or until chicken is opaque throughout when slashed in thickest portion.

Lift chicken to a warm serving platter; if any melted cheese remains in dish, spoon over chicken. Stir Sherry into pan juices; cook, uncovered, 1½ to 2 minutes until liquid is reduced and slightly thickened. Pour over chicken and garnish with parsley. Makes 2 servings.

Chicken Almond Sandwiches

Piquant blue cheese and almonds join the chicken in this hot sandwich filling. Make it ahead; then assemble the sandwiches just before heating.

  2 cups finely diced or shredded cooked chicken (see recipe for Baked Chicken Breasts on page 42)
  ¼ cup crumbled blue cheese
  3 tablespoons mayonnaise
  3 tablespoons thinly sliced green onion
  3 tablespoons chopped toasted almonds
  ½ teaspoon Dijon mustard
    Salt and pepper to taste
  6 French rolls or hamburger buns, split, toasted, and buttered

Lightly mix together chicken, cheese, mayonnaise, onion, almonds, mustard, and salt and pepper to taste. Cover and refrigerate if made ahead. To serve, spread filling evenly over bottom half of each bun. Close sandwiches and wrap each in paper toweling. Heat in the microwave oven, allowing 30 to 45 seconds for each sandwich. Let stand, wrapped, about 1 minute before serving. Makes 6 sandwiches.

Chicken with Wild Rice

Forty minutes from start to finish gives you a delicious meal-in-a-dish. While it cooks, put together a crisp salad of assorted greens, sliced cucumbers, mild onion rings, and cherry tomatoes, dressed with oil and vinegar.

- 1 package (6 oz.) brown and wild rice mix
- ¼ pound mushrooms, sliced
- 1⅓ cups hot water
- ¼ cup dry Sherry or additional water
- 2 pounds chicken breasts and thighs
  Paprika

In a 7 by 11-inch baking dish, combine the rice and all but 1 tablespoon of the rice seasoning mix, mushrooms, water, and Sherry. Cover and cook in microwave oven 15 minutes.

Meanwhile, rub remaining seasoning mix over chicken pieces. Stir rice and arrange chicken, skin side up, in a single layer over top. Sprinkle with paprika. Cover and cook for 12 to 15 minutes or until meat is no longer pink near bone when slashed; turn dish once or twice. Let stand, covered, for about 5 minutes. Makes 4 servings.

Chicken and Rice Espana

Exotically seasoned rice, studded with spicy sausage bits and peas, complements this juicy baked chicken. A salad of crisp greens and citrus could complete the menu.

- 2 cups quick-cooking rice
- 1 package (1½ oz.) Spanish rice seasoning mix
- 5 to 6 ounces linguisa sausage (casing removed), thinly sliced
- 1 cup frozen peas
- 1⅓ cups hot water
  About 2 pounds chicken legs and thighs (attached)
  Garlic salt, pepper, and paprika

In a shallow baking dish (about 9 inches square), combine rice, seasoning mix, linguisa, peas, and water. Arrange chicken pieces in a single layer over the rice mixture with skin side of thighs up and meatiest portions near edge of dish; sprinkle lightly with garlic salt, pepper, and paprika. Cover and cook in microwave oven 18 to 22 minutes, turning dish 2 or 3 times until meat near bone is no longer pink when slashed. Let stand, covered, about 5 minutes before serving. Serves 4.

Barbecue Chicken with Bananas

For this dish, choose firm, green-tipped bananas that will hold their shape when briefly cooked.

- 4 whole chicken legs (drumsticks and thighs attached)
- ⅓ cup catsup
- 1 tablespoon *each* brown sugar, vinegar, prepared mustard, salad oil, and instant minced onion
- 2 green-tipped bananas, cut in ½-inch slices

Rinse chicken; pat dry. Place in a shallow baking dish (about 7 by 11 inches). Combine catsup, brown sugar, vinegar, mustard, oil, and onion. Spoon about ⅔ of the sauce over chicken. Cook in the microwave oven, uncovered, 10 minutes; turn dish several times. Add bananas, spoon over remaining sauce, and cook, uncovered, for 3 minutes longer or until meat near bone is no longer pink when slashed. Let stand 2 to 3 minutes before serving. Serves 4.

Cheddar Chicken with Cracked Wheat

Cook the chicken a day or so ahead if more convenient; then cover and refrigerate meat and juices. Finish the casserole just before serving.

- About 3-pound broiler-fryer chicken, cut-up
  Water
- 1 chicken bouillon cube
- 2 tablespoons butter or margarine
- ¼ pound mushrooms, sliced
- ½ cup bulgur wheat
- 2 tablespoons instant minced onion
- ½ teaspoon dry rosemary
  Garlic salt and pepper
- 1½ cups shredded Cheddar cheese
  Paprika

In a shallow 7 by 11-inch baking dish, arrange chicken pieces in a single layer with meatiest pieces along outside edges (reserve giblets and neck for other uses). Cook in the microwave oven, uncovered, for about 18 minutes or until thigh meat is no longer pink near bone when slashed. Turn dish several times. Lift out chicken and set aside; drain juices into a 2-cup glass measure, skim and discard fat, and add enough water to make 1¼ cups total. Add bouillon cube and cook, uncovered, about 1 minute, stirring often, until dissolved.

Melt butter 1 minute in the baking dish; add mushrooms and cook, uncovered, 2 minutes. Stir in bulgur wheat, onion, rosemary, and chicken broth. Cover and cook about 8 minutes or until wheat is tender to bite and liquid is absorbed.

Meanwhile, remove and discard bones and skin from chicken; tear meat into bite-size pieces. When wheat is tender, stir in chicken and season to taste with garlic salt and pepper. Distribute cheese over top and sprinkle with paprika. Cook, uncovered, until cheese melts (2 to 3 minutes). Makes 4 servings.

Chile Chicken Burritos

Here's another idea for using Baked Chicken Breasts (recipe on page 42). These burritos are mild. You may want to pass bottled taco sauce.

- 2 **cups cubed cooked chicken**
- 2 **tablespoons** *each* **seeded, chopped, canned California green chiles and finely chopped onion**
- 1 **cup shredded jack cheese**
- 2 **tablespoons sour cream**
- ½ **teaspoon salt**
- 6 **flour tortillas (about 8 inches in diameter)**

Lightly mix chicken, green chiles, onion, cheese, sour cream, and salt. Spread about ½ cup down the center of each tortilla; then roll it into a cylinder. Wrap lightly in a paper towel and heat in the microwave oven 30 to 45 seconds for each burrito until filling bubbles. Let stand 1 minute before serving. Makes 6 burritos.

Turkey Teleme

Smooth, creamy teleme cheese and bright green peas blend with the turkey juices for a simple, delicious sauce. You serve it with boned turkey breast meat.

- ½ **turkey breast (3 to 3½ lb.), thawed if frozen**
  Ground nutmeg, salt, and pepper
- 1 **package (10 oz.) frozen peas**
- ⅓ **cup sliced green onion**
- 2 **teaspoons** *each* **cornstarch and water**
- ¼ **teaspoon grated lemon peel**
- 6 **ounces teleme cheese, sliced**

To bone half turkey breast, place it on a board, skin side down. Locate wishbone splinter, slip a sharp knife underneath, and cut bone away from meat. Then run knife blade along the length of the breast bone, cutting meat free while pulling bone away with your hand. Continue cutting down around rib cage, keeping knife close to bone until ribs are free. Locate wing socket, cut it out, and run blade along attached bones to free meat. Pull off skin.

Place meat in a serving dish (about 7 by 11 inches). Sprinkle lightly with nutmeg, salt, and pepper. Cover and cook in the microwave oven 10 to 12 minutes or until meat is no longer pink when slashed. Turn meat over and rotate dish once or twice during cooking.

Meanwhile, place peas in a colander and rinse with hot tap water until thawed; drain well.

Drain off all liquid from turkey into a 2-cup glass measure. Distribute peas and onions around meat.

Blend cornstarch and water, stir into pan drippings, and cook in glass measure, uncovered, for 1½ to 2 minutes or until bubbly and thickened; stir several times. Stir in lemon peel and salt and pepper to taste. Pour over meat and vegetables.

Arrange cheese slices over meat and cook, uncovered, about 2 minutes or until cheese is melted. Stir gently to combine melted cheese that flows off meat with vegetables and juices. To serve, cut thin slices across turkey breast and spoon vegetables and juices over top. Makes 4 to 6 servings.

Turkey Tortilla Casserole

For a Mexican fiesta in minutes, make up this casserole ahead and refrigerate it. Allow 4 to 6 minutes to reheat it in the microwave.

- 2 **tablespoons butter or margarine**
- 1 **medium-size onion, finely chopped**
- 1 **package (1⅝ oz.) enchilada sauce mix**
- 1 **can (6 oz.) tomato paste**
- 3 **cups hot water**
- 8 **corn tortillas, cut in shreds**
- 6 **to 7 cups cooked turkey meat (see Baked Turkey Breast recipe on page 43), cut in bite-size pieces**
- 1 **can (2¼ oz.) sliced ripe olives, drained**
- 2 **cups shredded Longhorn Cheddar cheese**
- ¼ **cup turkey broth**

Melt butter in a 7 by 11-inch baking dish in the microwave oven. Add onion and cook, uncovered, for 4 minutes or until limp; stir several times. Stir in enchilada sauce mix, tomato paste, and water; cook, uncovered, 8 minutes or until bubbly and thickened; stir often. Pour sauce into a bowl, leaving 2 or 3 tablespoons in the baking dish. Distribute about half the tortillas in dish, top with about half the turkey, then half the olives, half the sauce, and half the cheese. Repeat layers, ending with cheese.

Drizzle evenly with turkey broth. Cook, uncovered, 8 to 10 minutes or until hot through and cheese is melted. Makes about 8 servings.

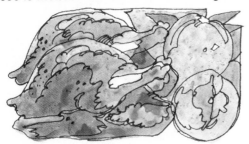

Rock Cornish Game Hens with Peaches

Often a good market buy, these miniature birds make a noteworthy entrée when baked on a bed of seasoned rice.

> 2 Rock Cornish game hens (20 to 24 oz. *each*), thawed
> 1 package (6 oz.) chicken-flavored rice mix
>   Water
>   About 3 tablespoons butter or margarine
> 1 can (1 lb.) cling peach halves
> 2 tablespoons honey
> 1 tablespoon dry mustard
> ¼ teaspoon curry powder
>   Paprika

Remove giblets from game hens; save for other uses. With poultry or kitchen shears, split hens in half, rinse well, and pat dry; set aside. In a 7 by 11-inch baking dish, combine contents of the seasoning packet from rice mix with water and butter called for on package. Cook, uncovered, in the microwave oven until hot (about 1 minute); stir in rice, cover, and cook 2 minutes.

Arrange hen halves in dish, skin side down, with meaty portions near edges of dish. Cover and cook 10 minutes, turning dish 2 or 3 times.

Meanwhile, drain peach halves, saving 2 tablespoons of the syrup. Set peaches aside. Combine reserved syrup, 1 tablespoon butter, honey, dry mustard, and curry powder in a small bowl. Cook, uncovered, until bubbly (about 45 seconds).

Lift out hen halves, stir rice well, and return meat to dish, skin side up. Brush skin evenly with honey mixture; cook 10 minutes longer or until meat near bone is no longer pink when slashed. Arrange peach halves around poultry. Brush with any remaining honey mixture and cook, covered, about 45 seconds. Sprinkle paprika over poultry and peaches. Let stand, covered, 5 minutes before serving. Serves 4.

Apricot-orange Glazed Duckling

Apricot jam contributes a mildly sweet, fruity accent to complement the richness of duck.

> About 5-pound ready-to-cook duckling, thawed
>   Pepper
> ½ cup apricot jam
> ⅓ cup regular-strength chicken broth
> 1 tablespoon soy sauce
> 1 tablespoon dry mustard
> 1 teaspoon grated orange peel
> 1 teaspoon *each* cornstarch and water

Remove giblets and neck from duck cavity; reserve for other uses, if you wish. Rinse duck well; then pat dry. Prick the skin in several places with a fork and sprinkle cavity and skin lightly with pepper. Secure wings akimbo style and fasten skin across neck opening to back with a wooden pick.

Place duck breast side down on a nonmetallic rack or inverted saucer in a 7 by 11-inch baking dish. Cook, uncovered, in the microwave oven for 10 minutes; turn dish once or twice.

Meanwhile, stir together the jam, broth, soy, mustard, and orange peel until well blended. Drain drippings from dish into a 2-cup glass measure; brush jam mixture generously over duck and cook, uncovered, for 10 minutes more, turning dish once or twice.

With two forks to support duck, tip and drain cavity juices into baking dish; turn duck breast side up. Cook, uncovered, for 10 minutes, turning dish once or twice. Drain drippings from baking dish into the glass measure, baste duck with remaining jam mixture, and cook, uncovered, 10 minutes longer or until leg joint moves easily. Drain juices from cavity into baking dish; place duck on serving platter and keep warm.

Combine all drippings in the glass measure; discard fat. Blend cornstarch and water, stir into drippings, and cook, uncovered, for 1 minute or until bubbly. Pass sauce. Serves 3 or 4.

Seafood

What a wave can do for a clam...

Treat yourself to an angler's delight: fish and shellfish emerging from a microwave oven moist and tender with their delicate flavor intact.

Fish steaks and fillets can be simply steam-poached without any additional liquid, butter-steamed with a variety of seasonings, or poached in liquid—such as wine or cream—when you want to serve the fish with a flavorful sauce.

Whole fish may be cooked the same way; but, as in conventional cooking or barbecuing, the thinner portions tend to overcook before the thick center section is done.

Shellfish come in their own cooking containers that respond magically to microwaves—clam and mussel shells open before your eyes, and raw, "green-shelled" shrimp, crab, and lobster turn pink.

The secret of properly cooking fish and shellfish is to watch them carefully—fish can overcook in a microwave oven in seconds. It's best to remove fish when barely done and then allow some "standing time" (see page 7) to finish the cooking. To insure more even cooking, arrange fish with thickest portions near the edges of the dish, turn over each piece about halfway through the cooking time, and turn the dish around several times.

Fresh fish generally gives better results than frozen fish. But thawed frozen fish can be satisfactorily prepared in a microwave oven, and the added moisture it gives up can be easily reduced to make a sauce.

Butter-steamed Fish

Fillets of white fish steam promisingly in a seasoned butter. If you use fish that was frozen, you can boil the liquid that accumulates in the baking dish until reduced and slightly thickened and then use it as a sauce for the cooked fish.

> 1 **pound fish fillets (sole, rockfish, or Greenland turbot), thawed if frozen**
> 2 **tablespoons butter or margarine**
>   **Seasonings (suggestions follow)**
>   **Salt and pepper**
>   **Parsley and lemon wedges**

Rinse fish and pat dry. In a 7 by 11-inch baking dish, melt butter with your choice of seasoning for 30 seconds in the microwave oven. Tip and tilt dish to evenly distribute butter. Arrange fish in a single layer, placing thicker portions toward outside of dish. Cook, covered, 2½ minutes; turn the fish over and cook 2 minutes until it flakes easily. Let stand, covered, 3 minutes. (If you use frozen fish, drain liquid from dish into a 2-cup glass measure; cook, uncovered, 3 minutes or until slightly thickened.)

Season with salt and pepper to taste. Spoon butter or reduced liquid over the fish; serve with parsley and lemon. Makes 2 to 3 servings.

Seasonings. Choose one of the following: ¼ teaspoon paprika or dill weed; 1 tablespoon chopped chutney and a dash cayenne; or ½ teaspoon grated lemon peel.

Creamy Dilled Fish Steaks

Fish bathes in cream as it cooks. You serve it in its own rich sauce accented with dill and Vermouth.

>   **About 2 pounds fish steaks, cut ¾ inch thick (halibut, swordfish, lingcod, sea bass, or salmon)**
> 2 **tablespoons butter or margarine**
> ¼ **teaspoon dill weed**
> 3 **tablespoons whipping cream**
> 1 **tablespoon dry Vermouth**
>   **Salt and pepper to taste**

Thaw fish and pat dry if frozen. In the microwave oven, melt butter with dill weed in a 7 by 11-inch baking dish until bubbly; stir in whipping cream and Vermouth. Arrange fish in a single layer and cook, uncovered, 3½ minutes. Turn fish over,

cover and cook 2 to 3 minutes until fish looks opaque throughout and flakes easily when probed with a fork. Season with salt and pepper. Serve immediately. Serves 4.

Fish with Mushroom Sauce

A dusting of nutmeg completes this very French dish of white fish masked with cheese, cream, mushrooms, and wine. Sauce and fish cook separately and then are united for a brief reheating.

> 6 **tablespoons butter or margarine**
> 1½ **pounds fish fillets (lingcod, Greenland turbot, halibut, giant sea bass, rockfish, or sole), thawed if frozen**
>   **White wine**
> ½ **pound mushrooms, thinly sliced**
> 3 **tablespoons all-purpose flour**
> ½ **cup half-and-half (light cream)**
>   **Ground nutmeg**
>   **Salt and pepper**
> ¾ **cup shredded Swiss cheese**

In a 7 by 11-inch baking dish, melt 2 tablespoons of butter in the microwave oven 30 seconds. Arrange fish in an even layer with thickest portions near edges of dish. Cover and cook 2½ minutes; turn fish over and cook, covered, 2 to 3 minutes or until opaque throughout. Lift out fish and set aside. Drain liquid into a measuring cup and add enough white wine to make 1 cup total; set aside.

Wipe out baking dish and add 2 more tablespoons butter. Cook 30 seconds or until melted. Stir in mushrooms and cook, uncovered, 4 minutes, stirring several times. Add remaining butter and flour and cook, stirring often, until bubbly. Gradually stir in wine mixture, half-and-half, and

⅛ teaspoon nutmeg; cook, uncovered, 3 to 4 minutes or until thickened, stirring often. Add salt and pepper to taste.

Arrange cooked fish in sauce; sprinkle cheese evenly over top and bake, uncovered, 2 minutes or until cheese melts. Dust very lightly with more nutmeg and serve. Makes 4 to 6 servings.

Sole Paupiettes with Lemon Sauce

Plump, elegant bundles of delicate sole fillets rolled around a savory crab mixture are bathed in a wine-lemon sauce. Choose a light, dry, white wine, such as Chablis or Chardonnay, to serve with the dish.

¾ **pound cooked crab, finely shredded**
1¼ **cups fine dry bread crumbs**
2 **eggs, slightly beaten**
6 **tablespoons lemon juice**
2 **tablespoons minced parsley**
½ **teaspoon** *fines herbes,* **or** ⅛ **teaspoon** *each* **thyme, oregano, basil, and rosemary leaves**
About ¼ teaspoon salt
Pepper
1½ **pounds small thin sole fillets**
½ **cup** *each* **dry white wine and regular-strength chicken broth**
Water
2 **tablespoons** *each* **butter or margarine and all-purpose flour**
Chopped parsley

Combine crab, crumbs, eggs, 4 tablespoons of the lemon juice, parsley, *fines herbes,* ¼ teaspoon salt, and pepper to taste. Evenly spoon mixture across the center of each fillet; fold sides over the filling, and roll fish to enclose. Secure with wooden picks. Place rolls side by side in a 7 by 11-inch baking dish; add wine and broth. Cook, covered, in the microwave oven 4 minutes or until fish flakes readily when probed with a fork; carefully turn fish over once. Transfer to a warm platter; cover and let stand. Strain cooking liquid into a glass measuring cup; add water, if needed, to make ¾ cup total liquid; set aside. Wipe out baking dish.

Melt butter in baking dish until bubbly; stir in flour, and cook, uncovered, 30 seconds. Gradually stir in cooking liquid; cook, uncovered, 4 minutes or until thickened, stirring once. Stir in remaining 2 tablespoons lemon juice, season to taste with salt and pepper, and pour sauce over fish rolls. Sprinkle with parsley. Serves 4 to 6.

Baked Fish with Vegetables

Peas and green pepper add their bright color to a creamy sauce to serve over lightly cooked fish. You can use rockfish, halibut, or Greenland turbot fillets or steaks.

2 **pounds fish fillets or steaks (about ½ inch thick), thawed if frozen**
¼ **cup butter or margarine**
¼ **pound mushrooms, sliced**
½ **cup finely chopped green pepper**
¼ **cup all-purpose flour**
½ **teaspoon salt**
¼ **teaspoon pepper**
Milk
1 **package (10 oz.) frozen peas, thawed**
1 **tablespoon lemon juice**
¼ **cup grated Parmesan cheese**

Arrange fish in an even layer in a 7 by 11-inch baking dish. Cover and cook in the microwave oven 3 minutes or until fish flakes easily when probed with a fork. Turn fish over and cook, covered, 2 to 3 minutes. Lift fish to a warm serving platter that has a rim. Pour liquid into a glass 2-cup measure and reserve.

Add butter to baking dish and cook 1 minute to melt. Add mushrooms and green pepper; cook, covered, 4 minutes, stirring once. Stir in flour, salt, and pepper; cook, uncovered, until bubbly (about 2 minutes). Add enough milk to fish liquid to make 1 cup total; gradually stir into vegetable mixture and cook, uncovered, 6 minutes or until thickened; stir often. Blend in peas and lemon juice, spoon over fish, and sprinkle with cheese. Return to oven and cook, uncovered, 1 minute or until heated through. Makes about 6 servings.

Salmon Steak Seattle

Whole salmon steaks bake in a spicy mixture of Worcestershire, paprika, and butter. Then they're offered with a western-style teriyaki sauce.

⅓ **cup butter or margarine**
½ **teaspoon salt**
¼ **teaspoon paprika**
1 **teaspoon Worcestershire**
6 **salmon steaks, cut ¾ inch thick (about 2½ lb.)**
1 **teaspoon prepared mustard**
2 **tablespoons soy sauce**
2 **tablespoons catsup**
1 **clove garlic, minced or pressed**

(Continued on next page)

In a 7 by 11-inch baking dish, melt butter in the microwave oven 1½ minutes. Add salt, paprika, and Worcestershire. Coat both sides of the salmon with the mixture and arrange in an even layer in baking dish, placing thickest pieces near edges of dish. Cook, uncovered, 3 minutes. Turn salmon over and cook, covered, 5 minutes or until fish flakes in thickest portion when probed with a fork. Remove salmon to a warm serving platter; cover and let stand. Skim fat from drippings and discard. Add mustard, soy sauce, catsup, and garlic to the drippings. Cook, uncovered, 1½ minutes or until bubbly. Pass in a bowl to spoon over the salmon. Makes 6 servings.

Oven-cooked Shrimp

Shrimp cooked in their shells are exceptionally moist and tender. Offer them warm or chilled as an appetizer or entrée with melted butter or your favorite cocktail sauce for dipping. Or use the cooked, shelled shrimp in salads and casseroles.

Arrange 1 pound medium-size (30 to 32 count) raw shrimp in a single layer on a large, flat, round plate with shrimp tails toward the center and meaty portions toward the outside edge. Cook, uncovered, in the microwave oven 3½ to 4½ minutes just until most of each shrimp turns pink; turn plate around once or twice. Let stand 3 to 5 minutes; then shell and devein. Makes about 2½ dozen appetizers or 3 to 4 main-dish servings.

Shrimp Foo Yung

For foo yung with a different flair, try this version that comes out as a single large omelet rather than as the small patties that restaurants often serve. You can mix in crab or slivers of cooked meat or chicken instead of shrimp—or just leave it at eggs and vegetables. (Cook about 1 minute less if no meat is used.)

>   2 tablespoons butter or margarine
>   4 eggs, well beaten
>   ½ pound fresh bean sprouts, rinsed and
>   drained
>   ⅓ cup thinly sliced green onions
>   1 cup (about 8 oz.) small cooked shrimp
>   ¼ teaspoon salt
>   ⅛ teaspoon *each* pepper and garlic powder
>   ¼ teaspoon liquid hot pepper seasoning
>   Soy sauce

In a 9-inch glass pie plate, melt butter in the microwave oven 30 seconds, tip and tilt dish to spread evenly. Stir together eggs, bean sprouts, onions, shrimp, salt, pepper, garlic powder, and hot pepper seasoning. Add to butter. Cook, uncovered, 5 minutes or until set to your liking, stirring every minute by pushing cooked mixture toward center of dish so liquid can flow to bottom and sides of dish. Serve with soy sauce to pass at the table. Makes about 4 servings.

Shrimp Jambalaya

This piquant creole dish cooks in less than half an hour in the microwave oven. For a spicier casserole, use three linquisa sausages and omit the ham.

>   2 tablespoons butter or margarine
>   1 large onion, chopped
>   ⅓ cup chopped green pepper
>   1 clove garlic, minced or pressed
>   1 can (1 lb.) tomato wedges in tomato juice
>   1 can (about 14 oz.) regular-strength chicken
>   broth
>   1 cup diced cooked ham
>   2 tablespoons chopped parsley
>   1 linquisa sausage (about 4 oz.), chopped
>   ¾ teaspoon salt
>   ¼ teaspoon thyme leaves, crumbled
>   Dash pepper
>   1 bay leaf
>   2 cups quick-cooking rice
>   1 pound medium-size shrimp (30 to 32
>   count), shelled and deveined

In a 3-quart casserole, melt butter in the microwave oven 1 minute until bubbly. Stir in onion, green pepper, and garlic; cover and cook 7 minutes or until vegetables are limp. Stir in tomatoes and their liquid, broth, ham, parsley, sausage, salt, thyme, pepper, bay leaf, and rice. Cover and cook 12 to 14 minutes, stirring 2 or 3 times, until rice is nearly tender. Arrange raw shrimp over top of rice; cover and cook 3 to 4 minutes or until shrimp turn pink. Let stand, covered, 5 minutes. Remove bay leaf, stir well, and serve in shallow soup bowls. Makes 4 to 6 servings.

Shrimp Curry with Rice

Cook the rice first; then pop all ingredients into the oven for 4 minutes. Presto—dinner is served!

- 6 **tablespoons butter or margarine**
- 1 **teaspoon curry powder**
- 2 **cloves garlic, minced or pressed**
- 1 **cup small cooked shrimp**
- ½ **cup thinly sliced green onion**
- ½ **cup chopped celery**
- ½ **cup sliced canned water chestnuts**
- 5 **tablespoons rice wine vinegar or 3 tablespoons white wine vinegar**
- ½ **teaspoon salt**
- 3 **cups cooked white or brown rice**

In a shallow 2-quart baking dish, melt butter in the microwave oven 1½ minutes. Stir in curry powder, garlic, shrimp, onion, celery, water chestnuts, vinegar, salt, and rice. Cover and cook 2 minutes; stir, turn dish, cover, and cook 2 minutes or until heated throughout. Makes 4 servings.

Dilled Shrimp and Cheese Buns

The filling is purposely dry until it heats; this keeps the bun from becoming soggy.

- 2 **cups small cooked shrimp or 2 cans (4½ oz. *each*) shrimp**
- ¾ **cup diced Swiss cheese**
- ¼ **cup sliced green onion**
- ½ **teaspoon dill weed**
- 2 **tablespoons mayonnaise**
- 1½ **teaspoons white vinegar**
  Salt and pepper
- 6 **hamburger buns, split, toasted, and buttered**

Coarsely chop shrimp; mix in cheese, onion, dill weed, mayonnaise, vinegar, and salt and pepper to taste. Spread mixture evenly over bottom bun halves; cover with bun tops. Wrap each sandwich lightly in paper and cook in the microwave oven, allowing 30 to 45 seconds for each sandwich or until cheese is melted. Makes 6 sandwiches.

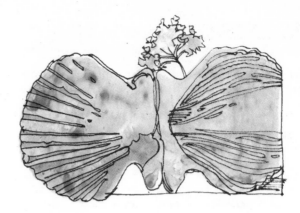

Coquilles St. Jacques in Cheddar Cheese Sauce

Served in a scallop shell, these tender scallops make an elegant first course or luncheon entrée. You can make them ahead and refrigerate; then reheat briefly before serving.

- 3 **tablespoons butter or margarine**
- ½ **pound mushrooms, sliced**
- 1 **pound scallops, cut in bite-size pieces**
- ½ **cup dry white wine**
- 2 **tablespoons all-purpose flour**
- ¼ **teaspoon salt**
- ½ **cup shredded Cheddar cheese**
  Chopped parsley or thinly sliced green onion

In a 7 by 11-inch baking dish, melt 1 tablespoon of the butter in the microwave oven 30 seconds. Add mushrooms and cook, uncovered, 4 to 5 minutes, stirring 2 or 3 times until limp. Lift out mushrooms and set aside; save liquid for other uses, if desired.

In the same dish, place scallops and white wine. Cover and cook 2½ minutes, stirring 2 or 3 times to cook evenly. Drain cooking liquid into a glass measuring cup (you should have about 1 cup) and set scallops aside with mushrooms.

In the same dish, melt the remaining 2 tablespoons butter 1 minute. Stir in flour and salt and cook, uncovered, 1 minute. Slowly stir in the 1 cup poaching liquid (add more white wine if needed to make 1 cup total). Cook 3 minutes, uncovered, or until thickened, stirring 2 or 3 times. Add cheese, stirring to mix in, and heat 1 minute or until melted. Add mushrooms and scallops to sauce and spoon mixture into 4 scallop shells or individual casseroles. (Cover and refrigerate at this point, if desired. To reheat, cook, uncovered, 1 to 2 minutes or until heated throughout.) Sprinkle with parsley and serve. Makes 4 main-course servings.

Poached Scallops in Wine

Scallops need special care in cooking, as they toughen quickly. Turn these every 30 seconds, moving inside chunks to outside positions. Serve them with the poaching liquid in individual scallop shells or ramekins, along with rice and a green vegetable.

1½ pounds scallops
½ cup dry white wine
2 tablespoons butter or margarine
2 tablespoons chopped parsley
  Paprika

Rinse scallops well; drain. Place them in a 7 by 11-inch baking dish; pour in the wine. Cover and cook in the microwave oven 3½ minutes, turning and stirring scallops 3 or 4 times. Cut scallops into large slices and distribute evenly in 4 scallop shells or ramekins. Pour the cooking liquid evenly over scallops.

In a small bowl, melt the butter 30 seconds. Spoon evenly over scallops. Sprinkle parsley over each serving; then dust with paprika and cook, uncovered, 30 seconds. Makes 4 servings.

Crab and Mushrooms Supreme on Muffins

For an elegant hot supper or brunch sandwich, sautéed mushrooms team up with a Sherried sour cream sauce and fresh crab meat to be spooned over toasted English muffins.

1 tablespoon butter or margarine
¾ pound mushrooms, sliced
1 tablespoon lemon juice
2 tablespoons dry Sherry
1 cup (½ pt.) sour cream
¾ pound fresh crab meat or 2 cans (7½ oz. *each*) crab meat
3 tablespoons grated Parmesan cheese
4 English muffins, split, toasted, and lightly buttered
1 tablespoon minced parsley

In a 7 by 11-inch baking dish, melt butter in the microwave oven 30 seconds. Add mushrooms and lemon juice; cook, uncovered, 4 minutes, stirring several times. Add Sherry and cook, uncovered, 6 minutes or until liquid is reduced by half. Stir in sour cream until well blended. Add crab and Parmesan cheese. Heat, covered, 3 minutes. Spoon crab sauce over muffins. Sprinkle with parsley for garnish. Makes 4 servings of 2 muffin halves each.

Cracked Crab and Turbot Stew

Dungeness crab and Greenland turbot cook together in this stew. When crab is out of season, you can make the meal entirely of turbot, using about 2 pounds.

1 large onion, finely chopped
1 tablespoon olive oil or salad oil
6 tablespoons catsup
1¼ cups regular-strength chicken broth
  About ½-inch piece cinnamon stick
¼ teaspoon thyme leaves
1½ teaspoons Worcestershire
2 thin lemon slices
1 pound Greenland turbot fillets (thawed if frozen), cut in about 1½-inch chunks
1 medium-size (about 1½ lb.) cooked Dungeness crab, cleaned and cracked
  Lemon wedges
  Salt to taste

In a 2-quart casserole, combine onion and oil; cover and cook in the microwave oven 4 to 5 minutes or until onion is limp, stirring 2 or 3 times. Add catsup, broth, cinnamon, thyme, Worcestershire, and lemon slices. Cover and cook 5 minutes, stirring several times. Remove cinnamon and lemon slices and discard. Place turbot chunks in sauce; then lay crab on top. Cover and cook about 3 minutes or until fish flakes when prodded. Let stand, covered, about 5 minutes. Ladle into wide, deep bowls; squeeze over the lemon, and add salt to taste. Serves 4.

Cracked Crab in Spicy Tomato Sauce

Finger food, messy and delicious, combines a spicy sauce and pieces of crab in the shell. Get out the napkins and bibs—and don't forget hot towels when the last shell is emptied.

1 cup catsup
½ cup hot water
2 whole cloves
½ teaspoon seasoned salt
¼ teaspoon *each* thyme leaves and sugar
1½ teaspoons Worcestershire
½ teaspoon prepared horseradish
½ bay leaf
1 large Dungeness crab (about 2 lb.), cleaned and cracked

In a 1½ to 2-quart baking dish, combine catsup, water, cloves, seasoned salt, thyme, sugar, Worcestershire, horseradish, and bay leaf. Cook in the microwave oven, uncovered, 2 minutes until it starts to bubble; stir once. Stir in crab pieces and heat through (about 2 minutes).

Eat crab with the sauce that clings to the shells; extra sauce may be served in small bowls. Makes 2 servings.

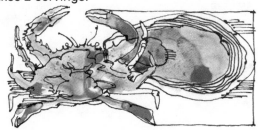

Turbot and Crab Casserole

Moderately priced Greenland turbot fillets (often labeled halibut) are generally available in supermarkets either frozen or thawed. The cooked fish has a flavor and texture similar to crab, making it a good extender for the more expensive seafood.

1 pound Greenland turbot fillets
2 tablespoons butter or margarine
¾ cup thinly sliced celery
¼ pound mushrooms, sliced
½ small green pepper, seeded and chopped
2½ tablespoons all-purpose flour
¾ cup milk
3 tablespoons dry Sherry
½ teaspoon savory leaves
1 teaspoon Dijon mustard
¼ teaspoon liquid hot pepper seasoning
⅛ teaspoon pepper
¼ pound crab meat
½ cup sliced water chestnuts
3 tablespoons grated Parmesan cheese
Chopped parsley

Arrange frozen or thawed turbot fillets in a 7 by 11-inch baking dish with thickest portions toward dish edges. Cover and cook in the microwave oven 4 to 6 minutes or until fish flakes when prodded (time will depend on whether fish is thawed or frozen). Lift out fish; drain well and break into bite-size pieces. Set aside. Save liquid for other uses, if desired.

Wipe out baking dish, add butter, and cook until bubbly. Stir in celery, mushrooms, and green pepper. Cover and cook 5 minutes or until mushrooms are limp, stirring several times. Blend in flour and cook 1 minute or until bubbly. Grad-ually stir in milk and cook about 3 minutes or until sauce is thickened, stirring often. Stir in Sherry, savory, mustard, hot pepper seasoning, pepper, crab, water chestnuts, and turbot. (Cover and refrigerate if made ahead.)

Cover and cook 2 to 3 minutes (about 4 minutes, if refrigerated). Uncover and sprinkle with cheese; cook 1 minute longer or until hot through. Garnish with parsley. Makes 4 servings.

Oysters with Pesto

Oysters open easily when you heat them briefly in the microwave oven. Serve them raw in the shell or follow this recipe, combining them with cheese, parsley, and basil for pesto sauce.

12 Eastern or 8 medium-size Pacific oysters
½ cup freshly grated Parmesan cheese
3 tablespoons minced parsley
1 tablespoon dry basil, crushed
2 tablespoons melted butter or margarine

Heat oysters in shells, uncovered, in the microwave oven about 2 minutes. Pry shells open and cut oysters free (leave in place in deeper shell, discarding other shell half). Arrange oysters in a 10-inch glass pie plate or shallow baking dish.

Combine cheese, parsley, basil, and butter to form crumbs; evenly distribute and pat firmly over oysters. Cook, uncovered, in the microwave oven for about 3 minutes or until oysters are piping hot and cheese mixture is bubbly around edges of shells. Turn plate around several times during cooking time. Makes 4 first-course servings of 2 or 3 oysters each.

Butter Oysters

Basil-dusted oysters, lightly cooked in butter and drizzled with wine, make a tantalizing meal opener.

2 tablespoons butter or margarine
1 jar (10 oz.) small Pacific oysters or 8 to 10 shucked Eastern oysters
All-purpose flour
½ teaspoon dry basil
1 tablespoon dry white wine

Place butter in a 7 by 11-inch baking dish; cook, uncovered, in the microwave oven 1½ to 2 minutes or until very bubbly.

(Continued on next page)

Meanwhile, pat oysters dry. Dip each in flour, shake off excess, and arrange in the butter; sprinkle with ¼ teaspoon of the basil. Cover lightly and cook 2 minutes; turn oysters over, sprinkle with remaining basil, cover lightly, and cook 2 minutes. Lift oysters and arrange in 3 or 4 individual serving dishes. Add wine to baking dish; stir until well blended and cook, uncovered, about 45 seconds. Spoon evenly over oysters and serve at once. Makes 3 or 4 first-course servings.

Hangtown Fry

Dating back to California gold rush days, this dish has many versions. All include eggs and oysters. The rest is up to the cook.

2 slices bacon, diced
⅓ cup chopped oysters (about 2 medium-size)
2 eggs
1 teaspoon water
Salt and pepper
Dash Worcestershire
Chopped green onion
Hot buttered toast

Place bacon in a 9-inch glass pie plate; cover and cook in the microwave oven for about 2 minutes or until almost crisp. Stir in oysters, cover, and cook 1 minute.

Meanwhile, beat eggs well with water, salt and pepper to taste, and Worcestershire. Stir into oysters, cover, and cook about 1½ minutes or until eggs are set to your liking; stir cooked portions into center several times to allow uncooked egg to flow to edges of pie plate. Turn out on a serving plate, garnish with chopped onion, and serve with hot buttered toast. Serves 1.

Clams with Garlic Butter

Steaming clams in the microwave oven are fascinating to watch. Put them in a dish and cover with plastic film; then see them pop open in 2 or 3 minutes. Offer garlic butter for dipping when the clams are ready.

¼ cup butter or margarine
1 small clove garlic, minced or pressed
1 tablespoon chopped parsley
1½ teaspoons lemon juice
1 dozen clams (or mussels) in their shells, well scrubbed

In a small serving bowl, place butter, garlic, parsley, and lemon juice. Cook in the microwave oven 1 minute or until butter is bubbly; set aside.

Place clams in a circle inside a glass pie plate or serving dish. Cover and cook about 3 minutes or until shells pop open. (Lift out opened clams and cook any that didn't open a little longer.) Serve with garlic butter. Makes 2 first-course servings.

Lobster Tails

Lobster can be taken from freezer to table in minutes when you need a very special entrée. First, thaw frozen lobster electronically until meat can be freed from shell. Then cook briefly.

2 frozen lobster tails (8 to 9 oz. *each*)
4 tablespoons melted butter or margarine
1 tablespoon lemon or lime juice
Dash liquid hot pepper seasoning
¼ teaspoon dry basil or ⅛ teaspoon ground cumin
Chopped parsley

To thaw frozen lobster tails, place shell side down, in a 7 by 11-inch baking dish with meatiest portions toward edges. Cover and cook in the microwave oven 1 minute. Let stand 1 minute; then turn shell side up; cover and cook 1 minute. Let stand, covered, 5 to 10 minutes or until meat is pliable.

Use kitchen scissors to cut along the underside of thawed lobster tail shells, clipping off the many fins along the outer edges.

Peel back the soft undershell and discard. Bend shell back, cracking some joints to prevent curling. Starting at thickest end, pull meat free in one piece with your fingers. Turn meat over in shells so rounded side is up. Place shells, meat side up, back in baking dish. Combine butter, lemon juice, hot pepper seasoning, and basil; brush generously over lobster. Cover and cook 2 minutes. Baste with more butter. Turn dish around, and cook, covered, 2 minutes. Baste again. Cover and cook 1 to 2 minutes or until meat is opaque throughout when slashed. Arrange on a serving dish, drizzle juices in baking dish over top, and garnish with chopped parsley. Offer any remaining butter to spoon over individual servings. Makes 2 servings.

Rice Is Nice

When barbecuing or broiling fish (or meat and poultry), put your microwave oven to use cooking a rice-vegetable dish.

Long grain rice takes almost as much time to cook in the microwave oven as it does on a conventional range top (see your manufacturer's manual for cooking times).

Quick-cooking rice, though, requires very little cooking time and can be combined with other interesting ingredients to serve alongside any entrée.

All these rice dishes reheat in about 3 minutes to their original moist state.

Rice Pilaf with Artichokes

The flavorful marinade from the canned artichoke hearts acts as a major seasoning ingredient in this rice dish. You might garnish it with toasted pine nuts or almonds just before serving.

2 jars (6 oz. *each*) marinated artichoke hearts
1 medium-size onion, chopped
1 clove garlic, minced or pressed
1 cup regular-strength chicken broth
1 cup quick-cooking rice
¼ cup chopped parsley
Salt and pepper

Drain artichokes, reserving 3 tablespoons of the marinade; set artichokes aside. In a 7 by 11-inch baking dish, place the 3 tablespoons marinade. Add onion and garlic and cook, uncovered, in the microwave oven 2½ minutes. Stir in broth, rice, parsley, artichokes, and salt and pepper to taste. Cover and cook 3 minutes, stirring once. Uncover and cook 1 minute more. Let stand, uncovered, 3 to 5 minutes. Makes 4 to 6 servings.

Rice Pilaf with Zucchini

Thin slices of zucchini dot this pilaf variation that's ready in a matter of minutes.

2 tablespoons butter or margarine
1 medium-size onion, finely chopped
3 cups thinly sliced zucchini
1 cup regular-strength beef broth
1 cup quick-cooking rice
¼ teaspoon *each* salt, pepper, and fines herbes
¼ cup grated Parmesan cheese

In a 7 by 11-inch baking dish, melt butter in the microwave oven 1 minute. Add onion and cook 2½ minutes, uncovered. Stir in zucchini and ¼ cup of the beef broth. Cook, covered, 5 minutes, stirring once. Stir in rice, remaining beef broth, salt, pepper, and fines herbes. Cover and cook 3 minutes. Stir in cheese and cook, uncovered, 1 minute. Makes 6 servings.

Cheddar Rice Casserole

To defrost the frozen spinach used in this colorful dish, use your microwave oven for the time suggested in your manufacturer's manual.

¼ cup butter or margarine
2 tablespoons chopped onion
1 cup quick-cooking rice
1 package (10 or 12 oz.) frozen chopped spinach, thawed and drained
1 tablespoon Worcestershire
½ teaspoon *each* marjoram and thyme leaves
4 eggs, slightly beaten
1 cup milk
2½ cups shredded sharp Cheddar cheese
Salt and pepper

In a deep 2 to 2½-quart baking dish, melt butter 2 minutes in the microwave oven. Add onion and cook, uncovered, 2 minutes. Stir in rice, spinach, Worcestershire, marjoram, thyme, eggs, milk, 2 cups of the cheese, and salt and pepper to taste. Cover and cook 6 minutes, stirring 3 or 4 times. Sprinkle remaining ½ cup cheese over casserole. Cook, covered, 4 minutes. Let set, uncovered, 5 minutes. Makes 6 servings.

Vegetables

Save vitamins, minerals, minutes

You'll be happily surprised at the way the microwave oven cooks vegetables. You can expect brilliant color and intense natural flavor every time.

Vegetables with a skin or husk—such as potatoes, squash, and corn on the cob—can be cooked in their natural coverings. (Pierce the skin or shell first to prevent steam pressure buildup and skin explosion.) Other whole vegetables, artichokes for instance, cook more quickly and evenly if you wrap them in clear plastic film or an oven roasting bag.

For a covered baking dish, choose a shallow wide one so the vegetables can be spread out. Arrange vegetables such as asparagus and broccoli with the tough stem ends toward the edges of the dish, tips toward the center. Turn the dish and stir occasionally for more even cooking. If the baking dish has no lid, you can use clear plastic film. Lift any cover off carefully away from you. That way you won't get burned by the escaping steam that has accumulated.

Fresh vegetables will vary in size and freshness, so cooking times are approximate and you'll want to check frequently for the doneness you prefer. Keep in mind that cooking will continue for a brief period after the vegetables are removed from the microwave oven.

Frozen vegetables cook with little or no additional liquid so there's a minimum of draining and more nutrients are retained. Add salt after cooking so vegetables keep their natural moisture. Even when reheated, the vegetables will have their original flavor and color and will not dry out, because the heat is generated internally.

Cream-glazed Artichoke Hearts with Basil

Cut off upper third from 18 artichokes (each about 1½ inches in diameter); trim off tough leaves, leaving only the tender, light-colored ones. Rinse artichokes well and cut each in half. In a 2-quart dish, cook 2 tablespoons butter or margarine and ½ teaspoon basil leaves for 1 minute in the microwave oven; add artichoke hearts, cover, and cook 4 to 6 minutes or until tender when pierced. Add 2 tablespoons whipping cream and salt and pepper to taste; cook, uncovered, until liquid is almost gone. Makes 2 or 3 servings.

Whole Artichokes

Cut off upper third of artichoke, remove tough outside leaves, and trim stem. With scissors, snip off prickly tips from all leaves, then rinse the artichoke well and wrap in clear plastic film. Cook medium-size artichokes (about 3½ inches in diameter) in the microwave oven as follows: 1 artichoke, 6 minutes; 2 artichokes, 8 to 9 minutes; 4 artichokes, 10 to 12 minutes, or until bottom of artichoke is tender when pierced. Serve with melted butter or mayonnaise.

Buttered Asparagus

Snap off and discard white fibrous ends from ½ pound of asparagus spears; rinse spears well. Arrange in a single layer, tips toward center, in a shallow baking dish. Add 1 tablespoon water. Cover and cook in the microwave oven 3 to 5 minutes until asparagus is just tender when pierced.

Let stand, covered, 3 to 5 minutes. Drain; season with salt and pepper to taste and about 1 tablespoon butter or margarine. Makes 2 servings.

For a 1½-pound bunch of asparagus, increase water to 2 tablespoons and cooking time to 7 to 9 minutes; turn dish once or twice. Let stand, covered, 5 minutes. Drain; season with salt and pepper to taste and 2 to 3 tablespoons butter or margarine. Makes 6 servings.

Butter-steamed Bean Sprouts

In a shallow 2-quart baking dish, melt 2 tablespoons butter or margarine in the microwave oven 1½ minutes, until bubbly. Stir in ½ pound fresh bean sprouts (about 3 cups), rinsed and drained. Cover and cook 3 minutes until the bean sprouts begin to wilt and look translucent. Let stand, covered, 3 to 5 minutes. Add salt and pepper to taste. Sprinkle with about 1 tablespoon chopped parsley. Makes 2 or 3 servings.

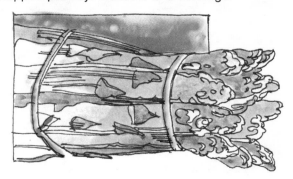

Broccoli-cheese Casserole

Chopped broccoli in a cheese-flavored custard goes well with roasted or barbecued beef, pork, or chicken.

- 2 packages (10 oz. *each*) frozen chopped broccoli
- ¼ cup (⅛ lb.) butter or margarine
- 1 large onion, chopped
- 2 tablespoons all-purpose flour
- ½ cup milk
- 1 jar (8 oz.) pasteurized process cheese spread
- 3 eggs, slightly beaten
- ¼ teaspoon *each* salt, pepper, and ground nutmeg
- ¾ cup finely crushed seasoned croutons

Place unopened packages of frozen broccoli in the microwave oven. Cook 4 to 5 minutes to defrost. Drain broccoli in a colander, pressing out all liquid. In a 2-quart casserole, melt butter 1½ minutes or until bubbly. Add onion and cook, uncovered, 2½ minutes or until tender. Stir in flour and cook, uncovered, 1 minute; then blend in milk and cook, uncovered, 1 minute or until thickened. Add cheese, stirring until melted. Blend in broccoli, eggs, salt, pepper, and nutmeg. Cook, uncovered, 3 minutes. Turn dish and stir gently, pushing cooked mixture from edges of dish to center for even cooking. Cook 3 minutes, then stir as before from outer edges to center. Sprinkle top evenly with crumbs. Cook, uncovered, 4 minutes or until mixture is set in center when lightly touched. Let stand, uncovered, 5 minutes before serving. Makes 6 servings.

Steamed Brussels Sprouts

Rinse 1 pound (about 2 dozen) Brussels sprouts. Cut off stem ends and remove any discolored outer leaves. Place sprouts in a 1½-quart baking dish with ¼ cup water. Cover and cook in the microwave oven 5 to 6 minutes or just until sprouts are tender, stirring once. Let stand, covered, about 5 minutes. Drain; season with about 2 tablespoons butter or margarine and with salt, pepper, and ground nutmeg to taste. Makes 4 servings.

Sesame Cauliflower Sauté

Generous amounts of parsley and green onion give color and freshness to this quickly cooked cauliflower dish.

1 small head (about 1 lb.) cauliflower
2 tablespoons sesame seed
2 tablespoons butter or margarine
1 tablespoon instant minced onion
½ cup water
¼ cup sliced green onions
2 tablespoons chopped parsley
   Salt and pepper
   Lemon wedges

Discard leaves and break cauliflower into flowerets. Cut each floweret through the stem into ¼-inch slices; set aside.

Place sesame seed in a 7 by 11-inch baking dish. Cook, uncovered, in the microwave oven 3 to 4 minutes or until golden; set seed aside.

In the same dish melt butter 1 minute. Add instant minced onion, cauliflower, and water. Cover and cook 3 minutes, stirring once or twice, or until cauliflower is just tender when pierced. Stir in green onions, parsley, sesame seed, and salt and pepper to taste. Cook, uncovered, 1½ minutes to blend flavors; stir once or twice. Serve with lemon wedges to squeeze over. Makes 4 servings.

Buttered Cauliflower

Remove outer leaves and trim core from 1 head cauliflower (about 1½ lb.). Trim off any brown or discolored spots. Place cauliflower in a clear roasting bag with 2 tablespoons water. Seal end with tape or string. With a fork, pierce top of bag in several places. Cook in the microwave oven for 8 to 10 minutes until cauliflower is tender in the center when pierced. Let stand in bag 5 minutes. Remove from bag, drain, and place in a serving dish; leave whole or break into flowerets. Season with 2 to 3 tablespoons butter or margarine and with salt, pepper, and dill weed to taste. Makes 6 servings.

Sweet and Sour Red Cabbage

Shred 1½ pounds red cabbage. Place in a 3-quart baking dish with 1 tart apple (peeled, cored and diced), 1 tablespoon butter or margarine, and 5 tablespoons red wine vinegar. Cover and cook in the microwave oven 18 to 22 minutes until cabbage and apples are tender, stirring 3 or 4 times. Stir in 1 teaspoon salt and 3 tablespoons sugar. Cover and cook about 5 minutes until liquid boils vigorously. Makes 6 servings.

Use full power setting on all recipes unless otherwise indicated

Steamed Carrots

Peel 6 medium-size carrots (about 1 lb.). Wrap them in clear plastic film or place them in a clear roasting bag, sealing the end with string. With a fork, pierce bag in 2 or 3 places. Cook in the microwave oven for 7 to 9 minutes until carrots are tender when pierced through the wrap or bag. Let stand, wrapped, 3 to 5 minutes. Cut carrots as you wish; season with 2 to 3 tablespoons butter or magarine and with salt and pepper to taste.

Puréed Celery Root

Peel and dice a 1-pound celery root. Place in a 1½ to 2-quart baking dish with ¼ cup warm water and 1 tablespoon lemon juice; stir. Cover and cook in the microwave oven 7 to 9 minutes or until tender when pierced, stirring once or twice. Let stand, covered, 5 minutes; drain. In blender container, place 1 tablespoon soft butter or margarine, 2 tablespoons milk or half-and-half (light cream), and cooked celery root. Whirl until smooth. Season purée to taste with salt, white pepper, and ground nutmeg. Reheat in serving dish, if necessary. Makes 2 or 3 servings.

Celery Root Sauté

Peel and dice 1 small celery root (you should have about 2 cups). Combine 2 tablespoons butter or margarine and ½ teaspoon paprika in a 1½ to 2-quart dish. Cook butter mixture in the microwave oven 1 minute. Stir in celery root; cover and cook for 5 minutes. Stir and cook, uncovered, for 1 to 2 minutes longer or until tender to bite. Season with salt and pepper and serve with lemon wedges to squeeze over. Makes 2 or 3 servings.

Sesame Chard

Prepare and cook Swiss chard or chard cabbage as in recipe for Chard with Cream Cheese Sauce (recipe follows). Omit cream cheese and salt; instead sprinkle lightly with toasted sesame seed and season to taste with soy sauce. Makes about 4 servings.

Chard with Cream Cheese Sauce

Break apart 1 large bunch (about 1 lb.) Swiss chard or 1 small head chard cabbage (also called bok choy); rinse well. Thinly slice white stems; separately slice green tops. In a 2½ to 3-quart dish, melt 2 tablespoons butter or margarine in the microwave oven for 1 minute. Add chard stems; cover and cook 5 minutes.

Uncover, stir in green tops, and cook, uncovered, 4 to 5 minutes or until tender to bite.

Clear a small area in dish; place in it 1 small package (3 oz.) cream cheese with chives, cut into small pieces; quickly mash with a spoon until melted. Tilt dish to drain juices into cheese; blend smoothly, then mix with chard. Cook, uncovered, 15 to 30 seconds and season to taste with salt and pepper. Makes about 4 servings.

Corn on the Cob

Be sure corn is completely enclosed in husk, and secure ends with string or rubber band. (Or remove husk and silk and wrap each ear individually in plastic film—this seems to make cooking a little more uniform.) Cook in the microwave oven 2½ to 3 minutes for each ear, until husk becomes bright green or kernels are tender when pierced; turn corn over once. Let stand, wrapped, 2 to 3 minutes. Then remove husk and silk. Offer butter, salt, and pepper at the table.

Jerusalem Artichokes (Sun Chokes)

Scrub 1 pound Jerusalem artichokes; do not peel. Cut across in ⅛ to ¼-inch slices. Combine 2 tablespoons butter or margarine and 1 teaspoon lemon juice in a shallow 2-quart baking dish. Cook in the microwave oven 1 minute. Stir in artichokes; cover and cook for 12 to 14 minutes or until tender to bite. Stir several times. Season to taste with salt and pepper and garnish with chopped parsley. Serves 4.

Sautéed Mushrooms

Rinse and pat dry ½ pound mushrooms; cut them through the stems into about ⅛-inch slices. Combine 2 tablespoons butter or margarine and ¼ teaspoon tarragon leaves in a 1-quart dish; cook, uncovered, in the microwave oven 1 minute. Stir in mushrooms; cover and cook 2 minutes. Uncover, stir in 2 to 3 tablespoons chopped green onions, and cook, uncovered, until most of the liquid is gone (4 to 6 minutes). Stir several times. Season to taste with salt and pepper. Makes 2 or 3 servings.

Mustard Greens with Bacon

Dice 4 slices bacon, place in a 3-quart dish, cover with a paper towel, and cook 2½ minutes in the microwave oven. Add ¼ cup finely chopped onion; cover and cook for 4 minutes or until bacon is crisp. Discard all but about 1½ tablespoons of the drippings.

Meanwhile, rinse and coarsely chop 1 bunch (about ¾ lb.) mustard greens; stir into bacon-onion mixture and cook, covered, 1½ to 2 minutes or until tender crisp. Season with salt and pepper to taste. Makes 3 or 4 servings.

Baked Onions

Peel 6 small yellow onions (2 to 2½ inches in diameter). Cut a thin slice from root end of each so onions will stand upright. Cut into stem end to make small cone-shaped hole. Arrange onions in a circle in a glass pie plate or shallow round serving dish. Fill hollowed-out cones with soft butter or margarine. Cover lightly and cook in the microwave oven 6 to 10 minutes or until tender when pierced. Let stand, covered, about

5 minutes. Season with salt, pepper, and paprika. Makes 6 servings.

Buttery Sage Onions

Peel small white boiling onions (1 to 1½ inches in diameter). Arrange about 1 inch apart in a 1 to 2-quart dish; dot each with ½ to 1 teaspoon butter or margarine and sprinkle lightly with rubbed sage. Cover and cook in the microwave oven as follows: 4 onions, 4 to 5 minutes; 6 onions, 6 minutes; 12 onions, 9 to 10 minutes—or until tender when pierced. Season to taste with salt and pepper. Allow 3 or 4 onions per serving.

Edible-pod Peas with Water Chestnuts

Snap off ends and remove strings from 1 pound edible-pod peas; rinse. In a 2 to 3-quart dish, melt 2 tablespoons butter or margarine in the microwave oven 1 minute. Stir in peas; cover and cook 2 minutes. Remove cover, stir in ½ cup sliced canned water chestnuts, and cook, uncovered, until peas are just tender to bite (about 4 minutes). Season with soy sauce and pepper to taste. Serves 4.

Red Bell or Green Peppers

Remove stem end and seeds from 4 medium-size peppers; rinse and cut into ¼-inch strips. In a 2-quart dish, heat 1 tablespoon olive oil and 1 tablespoon butter or margarine in the microwave oven 1 minute or until hot. Stir in pepper strips; cover and cook 2½ minutes. Uncover, season to taste with garlic salt and pepper, and cook, uncovered, for 1 to 2 minutes or until peppers are tender to bite. Makes 6 to 8 servings.

To precook peppers for stuffing, remove stem end and seeds from 2 medium-size peppers. Rinse, place in a dish, cover with clear plastic film, and cook for 3 minutes. Remove and let stand, covered, for about 5 minutes; then stuff with your favorite cooked mixture.

Au Gratin Potatoes

A sprinkling of nutmeg adds a subtle flavor to this casserole of thinly sliced potatoes, Swiss cheese, and creamy custard.

  2 **pounds (5 to 6 medium-size) new potatoes, peeled**
    Salt, pepper, ground nutmeg, and garlic salt
1½ **cups shredded Swiss cheese**
  ½ **cup whipping cream**
  1 **egg yolk, slightly beaten**

Cut potatoes into very thin slices. Arrange about ⅓ of the potatoes in a greased 2½ to 3-quart baking dish; sprinkle lightly with salt, pepper, nutmeg, and garlic salt, and then with ½ cup of the cheese. Repeat layers until all potatoes and cheese are used. Heat whipping cream in a glass measuring cup in the microwave oven about 1¼ minutes or until it begins to bubble. Gradually stir hot cream into beaten egg yolk. Pour cream mixture over potatoes. Cover and cook 15 to 20 minutes, stirring lightly several times, until potatoes are tender to bite. Let stand, covered, 5 minutes. If you wish, uncover casserole and place it under the broiler of your conventional oven for a few minutes to brown top lightly. Makes 6 servings.

Baked Potato

Scrub 1 small to medium-size baking potato. Pierce it with a fork in 2 or 3 places. Place on paper towel and cook in the microwave oven for 4 to 5 minutes; turn potato over once or twice and reposition in oven during cooking. Let stand, uncovered, about 2 minutes before cutting open. To serve, top with butter, margarine, or sour cream, and salt and pepper to taste. Serves 1.

Baked New Potatoes

Scrub medium-size red or white new potatoes (about 4 to 5 oz. *each*). Pat them dry and pierce each in several places with a fork. Place potatoes several inches apart on 1 or 2 paper towels and cook, uncovered, in the microwave oven as follows: 2 potatoes, 6 minutes; 4 potatoes, 8 to 9 minutes; 6 potatoes, 10 to 12 minutes—or until potatoes are tender when squeezed; turn potatoes over once or twice and reposition in oven during cooking.

To serve hot, split and season to taste with butter or margarine, salt, and pepper; or with chive-seasoned sour cream. Or let them cool, peel (if desired), and slice or dice for potato salad.

Baked Sweet Potatoes or Yams

Scrub medium-size sweet potatoes or yams (about 8 oz. *each*); pat dry. Pierce each in several places with a fork. Arrange on paper towel in the microwave oven and cook, uncovered, as follows: 1 potato, 5 to 6 minutes; 2 potatoes, 8 to 11 minutes; 3 potatoes, 12 to 15 minutes; 4 potatoes, about 18 minutes—or until potatoes are soft when squeezed. Turn potatoes over once or twice and reposition in oven during cooking.

To serve, cut crisscross slashes in each potato and squeeze to expose interior. Season each potato with about 1 tablespoon butter or margarine and sprinkle lightly with ground cinnamon and cloves.

Baked Acorn Squash with Ginger Butter

Pierce a 1½ to 2-pound acorn squash in several places with a fork. Place on paper towel in the microwave oven and cook, uncovered, 4 minutes. Then turn squash over and cook, uncovered, 4 to 6 minutes or until surface gives under pressure.

In a glass measuring cup combine 3 tablespoons butter or margarine, 2 tablespoons honey, 1 tablespoon lime juice, and ½ teaspoon ground ginger. Cook, uncovered, 1½ minutes or until bubbly.

Cut squash in half lengthwise and scoop out and discard seeds and membrane; place, cut side up, in a shallow baking dish. Spoon butter mixture evenly over cut surfaces and sprinkle lightly with cayenne; cook, uncovered, 1 to 2 minutes, basting once with any remaining butter. Makes 2 servings.

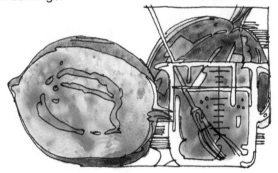

Baked Spaghetti Squash

On the outside, spaghetti squash looks much like any other winter squash. But after cooking it you find the flesh is made up of long, slightly crisp, spaghetti-size strands. Serve squash from the shell, seasoned with flavored butter.

Pierce a 3½ to 4-pound spaghetti squash with a fork in several places. Place on paper towel in the microwave oven and cook, uncovered, 15 minutes, turning squash over 3 or 4 times. Let stand, uncovered, 3 to 5 minutes. Surface of the squash should give under pressure. If it doesn't, cook 2 to 4 minutes longer.

To serve, split squash lengthwise. Scoop out and discard seeds; with a fork, pull strands free from shell. Toss with a flavored butter (suggestions follow) until evenly coated, and serve in the shell. Makes 6 to 8 servings.

Herb-cheese Butter. Blend together ½ cup (¼ lb.) soft butter or margarine, 3 tablespoons finely chopped parsley, ½ teaspoon Italian herb seasoning (or ¼ teaspoon *each* dry basil and marjoram leaves), ¼ teaspoon *each* garlic salt and pepper, and ¼ cup grated Parmesan cheese.

Spiced Butter. Blend together ½ cup (¼ lb.) soft butter or margarine, 3 tablespoons firmly packed brown sugar, ¼ teaspoon *each* ground cinnamon and allspice, and ⅛ teaspoon ground nutmeg.

Butter-steamed Turnips

Peel 1 bunch (5 or 6) medium-size turnips. Cut in about ¼-inch-thick slices. Arrange in an even layer in a 1½ to 2-quart baking dish. Add 2 tablespoons water and then dot with 2 tablespoons butter or margarine. Cover and cook in the microwave oven 7 to 9 minutes, stirring once or twice, until turnips are just tender when pierced. Let stand, covered, 3 to 5 minutes. Drain; season with salt and lemon pepper to taste, and garnish with finely chopped parsley or green onions. Makes 4 servings.

Vegetable Pie

A crustless vegetable custard pie makes a satisfying lunch or supper entrée. Cut in generous wedges and pass unflavored yogurt at the table to spoon over each serving.

 1 tablespoon butter or margarine
 1 package (10 or 12 oz.) frozen chopped spinach
 2 eggs
 3 egg yolks
1¼ cups skim milk
 2 tablespoons all-purpose flour
 1 teaspoon salt
 ¼ teaspoon *each* pepper and ground nutmeg
 1 cup thinly sliced green onions
 1 cup chopped iceberg lettuce
 ¼ cup chopped parsley
  About ½ cup unflavored yogurt

In a 9-inch pie plate, melt butter 1 minute in the microwave oven; tip plate to coat bottom and sides with butter, then set aside.

Place unopened package of spinach in the microwave oven and cook 3 minutes or until package is pliable. Place thawed spinach in a colander and press out all excess liquid.

Stir together eggs, egg yolks, skim milk, flour, salt, pepper, and nutmeg. Stir in drained spinach, onions, lettuce, and parsley. Pour mixture into buttered pie plate. Cook, uncovered, 4 minutes. Stir gently, pushing cooked mixture from edges into center of pie plate. Cook, uncovered, 6 to 7 minutes more or until pie is firm in middle when gently shaken, stirring (as before) every 2 minutes. Let stand, uncovered, 5 minutes. Cut in wedges and pass unflavored yogurt to spoon over individual servings. Makes 6 servings.

Desserts

Cakes and cookies, pies and puddings

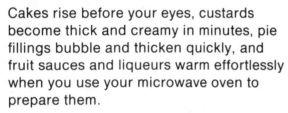

Cakes rise before your eyes, custards become thick and creamy in minutes, pie fillings bubble and thicken quickly, and fruit sauces and liqueurs warm effortlessly when you use your microwave oven to prepare them.

Cakes and bar cookies cook so quickly there's little or no browning, but it's no problem with a batter that is naturally dark, such as chocolate or spice. The pale appearance of other batters can be disguised with a topping or frosting. Toppings can also hide the uneven surface that can sometimes occur in microwave cake baking.

Use wax paper to line the bottom of the baking dish if you plan to remove the whole cake from the dish before serving. Do not grease or flour the baking dish; doing so tends to cause a dense layer to form on the bottom of the cake.

Cook cakes just until a wooden pick inserted in the center comes out clean. The top may still be slightly moist, but it will become set and dry as it stands outside the oven, since cooking continues for a brief period. Overcooking toughens a cake.

Pies present special challenges and special opportunities for the microwave user. Crumb crusts do very well in the microwave oven,

and we include a basic recipe for the crust in this chapter. You can also bake pastry pie shells electronically, but they lack color and frequently are tough and brittle. Therefore we recommend baking pastry pie shells in a regular oven. You can do the fillings in the microwave and then combine the two. Also use your microwave oven to reheat chilled fruit pies and warm breakfast pastries.

Puddings and custards can be baked without the usual water bath, but they need to be stirred frequently during cooking.

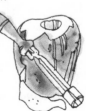

Breads do not fare well in the microwave oven. Loaves rise irregularly, are pale, and tend to be heavy and chewy. But the microwave is an easy, fast way to heat baked muffins, biscuits, or rolls, or to have warm, soft tortillas in seconds. Popovers, cream puffs, and angel food cakes (products that depend on eggs for leavening) should be baked in a conventional oven.

Fruits retain bright color and fresh flavor in an assortment of dessert ideas in this chapter. Cut fruits in uniform pieces and stir frequently for even cooking.

Date Crisp Cookies

Flakes of coconut coat crunchy date balls that are almost candy. Keep some on hand for an extra-sweet treat.

 1   **egg**
 6   **tablespoons sugar**
 ¾   **cup chopped pitted dates**
 ½   **teaspoon vanilla**
 1½ **cups ready-to-eat crisp rice cereal**
     About ¾ cup flaked coconut

In a 1½-quart mixing bowl or casserole, slightly beat egg. Stir in sugar, then dates. Cook, uncovered, in the microwave oven 2 to 3 minutes until dates are soft, stirring once or twice. Then stir mixture until it forms a paste (date skins will make it lumpy). Mix in vanilla and cereal.

Using two spoons, mold mixture into 1-inch balls. Put coconut on a plate or wax paper and roll each ball to coat all sides with coconut. Let cookies stand in a cool place 20 minutes until firm. Makes 2 dozen.

Honey Granola Bars

Quick-energy granola bars are great to pack along on a hike or picnic. Made with dried apricots or raisins, they keep well at room temperature when wrapped airtight.

Spread ¼ cup sesame seed in a 7 by 11-inch baking dish. Cook, uncovered, in the microwave oven about 5 minutes or until golden, stirring several times. Set seed aside.

In a 2 to 3-quart glass bowl without cover, cook ½ cup honey to boiling; then boil 1 minute. Blend ¾ cup chunk-style peanut butter into hot honey. Return to oven and cook, uncovered, 30 seconds. Mix together 3 cups granola (homemade or purchased; crush any large lumps), ½ cup chopped nuts (walnuts, almonds, or filberts), ⅓ cup chopped dried apricots, toasted sesame seed, and ¼ cup *each* toasted sunflower seed, toasted wheat germ, and coconut. Stir into hot honey mixture; then press mixture evenly into well-buttered 7 by 11-inch baking dish. Cover and chill at least 1 hour. Cut into bars about 1 by 2 inches. Makes about 3 dozen bars.

Variations. Use white corn syrup in place of honey. Substitute raisins for dried apricots.

Cheesecake Tarts

Creamy little individual cheesecakes, made in advance and chilled, save you any last-minute dessert worries. Spoon a dollop of fruit jam onto each cake just before you serve it.

 3   **tablespoons butter or margarine**
 ½   **cup graham cracker crumbs**
 1½ **teaspoons sugar**
 1   **large package (8 oz.) cream cheese (at room temperature)**
 ¼   **cup sugar**
 1   **egg**
 1   **teaspoon vanilla**
 6   **teaspoons berry or fruit jam**

In a glass mixing bowl, melt butter 1 minute in the microwave oven. Blend in graham cracker crumbs and the 1½ teaspoons sugar.

Line 6 glass custard cups with paper baking cups (about 2-inch diameter) and spoon crumbs equally into each cup. With a spoon, press crumbs firmly over bottom and up sides.

Beat together cream cheese and the ¼ cup sugar until smooth (if cream cheese is cold, remove foil and cook 30 seconds, uncovered, in the microwave oven). Add egg and vanilla; mix in well. Spoon mixture equally into crumb-lined cups.

Cook, uncovered, 1½ to 2 minutes, shifting inside cups to outside positions after 1 minute. Chill, uncovered, 1 hour (cover when cold if storing longer). At serving time, spoon 1 teaspoon berry or fruit jam onto each tart. Serves 6.

Dried Fruit and Nut Bars

Packed full of nuts, these fruit-flavored dessert bars can be rolled in powdered sugar to dress them up before serving.

 3 tablespoons butter or margarine
 2 eggs
 ½ cup firmly packed brown sugar
 ½ teaspoon vanilla
 ½ cup all-purpose flour (unsifted)
 ½ teaspoon *each* baking powder, salt, and grated orange peel
 1 cup chopped walnuts
 2 cups chopped dates or 1 cup chopped dates and ½ cup *each* chopped dried apricots and raisins
    Powdered sugar

Melt butter in a small cup in the microwave oven 1½ minutes or until bubbly; set aside. Beat eggs until foamy; then beat in brown sugar, vanilla, and butter. Mix together flour, baking powder, salt, and orange peel; stir into egg mixture. Then mix in nuts and dates. Spread batter in a buttered 8-inch-square baking dish and cook, uncovered, 6 to 7 minutes or until a wooden pick inserted in center comes out clean; turn dish three times. Cut into 1 by 2-inch bars while still warm. Roll in powdered sugar when cool, if desired. Makes about 32 bars.

Rocky-top Chocolate Squares

Moist, double-chocolate squares topped with chocolate-coated nuts and marshmallows make a fine coffee hour snack. Pudding mix and chocolate pieces are the shortcut secrets.

 ½ cup all-purpose flour (unsifted)
 ½ teaspoon baking powder
 9 tablespoons butter or margarine
 2 eggs
 ¼ cup sugar
 1 teaspoon vanilla
 2 packages (3¾ oz. *each*) regular chocolate fudge pudding and pie filling
 ½ cup *each* snipped pitted dates and flaked coconut
 1 package (6 oz.) semisweet chocolate pieces
 2 cups miniature marshmallows (lightly packed in cup)
 ½ cup chopped walnuts or pecans

Mix flour with baking powder; set aside. In a 1½ to 2-quart glass bowl, melt butter in the microwave oven 1 minute. In the large bowl of an electric mixer, beat eggs until frothy; then beat in sugar until well blended. Add vanilla and 6 tablespoons of the melted butter. With mixer on low speed, mix in flour mixture and pudding mix until well blended. Then stir in dates and coconut. Spoon into an 8-inch-square baking dish. Cook, uncovered, 5 to 6 minutes or until a wooden pick inserted in center comes out clean; turn dish twice. Let cool 15 minutes.

Meanwhile, to the remaining 3 tablespoons melted butter, add chocolate pieces. Cook, uncovered, 30 seconds. Remove and stir until chocolate is melted and blended with butter. Add marshmallows and nuts; stir until completely coated with chocolate. Spoon topping evenly over partially cooled dessert. Cool completely and then cut into about 16 squares.

Make-ahead Granola Topping

You can make this healthful, crunchy topping from your own or a packaged granola. Keep it on hand to use on coffee cakes, on fruit pies, or as an ice cream topping.

Place 6 tablespoons butter or margarine in a large pie plate or shallow baking dish. Cook in the microwave oven about 3 minutes or until bubbly.

Stir in ⅔ cup firmly packed brown sugar, ⅓ cup finely chopped nuts, 1 teaspoon ground cinnamon, ¼ cup all-purpose flour, and 1 cup granola (crush any large lumps). Cook, uncovered, 4 to 5 minutes or until granola is toasted and flavors are well blended; stir once or twice. Remove from oven, allow to cool about 5 minutes, and then break up into smaller pieces. Cool completely; store in an airtight container. Makes 3 cups.

Crumb Pie Topping

Simple crumb toppings can add extra sweetness and crunchy texture to pies or puddings. Sprinkle this one over the baked dessert of your choice.

Combine ⅓ cup firmly packed brown sugar and ½ cup all-purpose flour. With 2 knives, cut in ¼ cup (⅛ lb.) butter or margarine until crumbly.

(Continued on next page)

Cook, uncovered, in a large pie plate in the microwave oven 2½ to 3 minutes or until bubbly throughout. Turn dish 2 or 3 times. Cool slightly; then mix with fork. Sprinkle on baked pies or puddings. Makes about 1 cup.

Basic Crumb Pie Shell

To make fine crumbs, whirl broken wafer-type cookies in a blender or crush them in a plastic bag with a rolling pin.

¼ cup butter or margarine
1¼ cups fine cooky crumbs (chocolate, vanilla, or lemon wafers; graham crackers; gingersnaps; or macaroons)
2 tablespoons sugar

Melt butter in a 9-inch pie plate in the microwave oven 1½ minutes or until bubbly. Combine crumbs and sugar and stir into butter until well blended. Evenly press crumb mixture against bottom and sides of pie plate. Cook, uncovered, 2 to 2½ minutes or until firm when touched; turn plate once. Let cool completely before filling. Makes a 9-inch pie shell.

Lemon Meringue Pie

Billowy meringue cooks to perfection in the microwave oven to crown this fresh-tasting, tangy pie.

1½ cups water
1½ cups sugar
7 tablespoons cornstarch
¼ teaspoon salt
3 egg yolks
3 tablespoons butter or margarine
2 teaspoons grated lemon peel
½ cup lemon juice
9-inch baked pastry shell
Meringue (recipe follows)

Cook water in the microwave oven 2 to 3 minutes or until simmering. In glass quart measure, blend sugar, cornstarch, and salt. Gradually pour hot water into sugar mixture, stirring well to eliminate all lumps. Cook, uncovered, 4 minutes or until very thick and bubbly; stir often (7 or 8 times). In a small bowl, beat egg yolks lightly. Gradually stir about 3 tablespoons hot mixture into yolks and then stir yolks back into hot mixture. Cook, uncovered, 1 minute longer, stirring once. Blend in butter, lemon peel, and lemon juice; cool. Pour into baked pastry shell.

Pile meringue onto cooled pie filling, making sure it touches crust all around. Cook, uncovered, 3 minutes, turning pie 4 times to cook evenly. Cool away from drafts; then refrigerate if desired. Makes 6 servings.

Meringue. With an electric mixer, beat 3 egg whites and ¼ teaspoon cream of tartar until frothy. At high speed gradually beat in 6 tablespoons sugar, 1 tablespoon at a time, until mixture is stiff and glossy (do not underbeat). Beat in 1 teaspoon lemon juice or ½ teaspoon vanilla.

Blueberry Pie

When you are in a hurry you can serve the fruit mixture as a pudding. Simply spoon the cooked pie filling into sherbet glasses and chill it. Then pass cream at the table to pour over each serving.

5 cups fresh or partially thawed unsweetened frozen blueberries
¾ cup sugar
4 tablespoons tapioca (or 3 tablespoons cornstarch)
½ teaspoon ground cinnamon
2 tablespoons lemon juice
1 to 2 tablespoons butter or margarine (optional)
9-inch baked pastry shell
Whipped cream (optional)

Combine berries, sugar, tapioca, and cinnamon in an 8-inch-square baking dish. Stir in lemon juice and let stand at least 10 minutes. Cook, uncovered, in the microwave oven for 10 minutes or until bubbly and thickened; stir 4 or 5 times. Stir in butter, if desired, and set aside to cool about 1 hour; then spoon into baked pastry shell. Cover and chill 3 to 4 hours. Serve topped with whipped cream, if desired. Makes 6 servings.

Fresh Peach Filling

You can vary the sugar and tapioca to suit the peaches you are using. For ripe, sweet, juicy fruit, use the smaller amount of sugar and the larger amount of tapioca for thickening. Fruit that is less ripe will require more sugar and, if not juicy, less tapioca.

5 cups sliced fresh peaches
1 tablespoon lemon juice
1 to 1¼ cups sugar
3 to 4 tablespoons quick-cooking tapioca
½ teaspoon ground coriander or cinnamon
1 to 2 tablespoons butter or margarine
    (optional)
    9-inch baked pastry shell
    Sour cream (optional)

Place sliced peaches in an 8-inch round or square baking dish. Stir in lemon juice. Combine sugar with tapioca and coriander; stir gently into peach slices and allow to stand about 10 minutes. Cook, uncovered, in the microwave oven 13 minutes or until mixture is bubbly and peaches are tender when pierced; stir 5 or 6 times. Add 1 to 2 tablespoons butter, if desired. Let cool about 1 hour; then spoon into baked pastry shell. Serve with dollops of sour cream, if desired. Makes 6 to 8 servings.

stir, and cook 8 minutes or until juices are bubbling and thickened; stir occasionally (apple slices should be almost tender when pierced). Remove from oven and allow to cool, uncovered, 20 to 30 minutes before spooning into baked pastry shell. Sprinkle with Granola Topping or chopped nuts, if desired. Chill thoroughly (overnight, if you like). Serve with whipped cream or ice cream, if desired. Makes 6 to 8 servings.

Sugarless Apple Pie

A surprise ingredient—frozen apple juice—sweetens apple pie the natural way.

1 can (12 oz.) frozen apple juice concentrate
3 tablespoons quick-cooking tapioca
⅛ teaspoon salt
1 teaspoon ground cinnamon
½ teaspoon ground nutmeg
    About 5 large Golden Delicious apples,
        peeled, cored, and sliced about ¼ inch
        thick (6 to 7 cups)
2 tablespoons butter or margarine
    9-inch baked pastry crust
1 cup Granola Topping (page 71) or ½ cup
    chopped nuts (optional)
    Whipped cream or ice cream (optional)

Defrost apple juice by removing both ends of can and pushing out frozen juice into an 8-inch-square baking dish. Cook, uncovered, in the microwave oven until juice is thawed. Stir in tapioca, salt, cinnamon, and nutmeg; allow to stand at least 10 minutes while preparing apples. Add butter and sliced apples to juice mixture. Cover and cook 8 minutes, stirring once or twice. Remove cover,

French Apple Pie

First cook the crumbly streusel topping; then sprinkle it over the cooled pie filling. You can use it on other fruit pies as well.

    Crumb Pie Topping (page 71)
6 cups thinly sliced tart apples, peeled
1 tablespoon lemon juice
¾ cup sugar
2 tablespoons quick-cooking tapioca
1 teaspoon ground cinnamon
¼ teaspoon ground nutmeg
2 tablespoons butter or margarine (optional)
    9-inch baked pastry shell

Prepare Crumb Pie Topping; set aside. Combine apples, lemon juice, sugar, tapioca, cinnamon, and nutmeg in a 7 by 11-inch baking dish; mix lightly. Let stand at least 10 minutes. Cook, uncovered, in the microwave oven 10 to 12 minutes or until apples are almost tender, stirring 3 times. Remove from oven and gently stir in butter, if desired. Cool 30 minutes before spooning into baked pastry shell. Sprinkle with Crumb Pie Topping. Makes 6 servings.

Blackberry Pudding

Serve this berry-filled cake warm, with a foamy Sherry Sauce to pour over top.

Wash 2 cups blackberries; drain well. Toss lightly with ¼ cup all-purpose flour and ½ teaspoon ground cinnamon; set aside.

Beat together ⅓ cup butter or margarine and 1 cup sugar until fluffy. Beat in 2 eggs, one at a time, beating until creamy and light. Stir together 1½ cups all-purpose flour (unsifted), 2 teaspoons baking powder, and ¼ teaspoon salt. Add to egg mixture alternately with ½ cup milk. Blend in ½ teaspoon vanilla.

Spoon about ⅓ of the batter evenly into an 8-inch-square baking dish; sprinkle with half the berries, then repeat with ⅓ dough, remaining berries, and remaining dough. Sprinkle top with a mixture of 2 tablespoons sugar and 1 teaspoon ground cinnamon. Cook, uncovered, in the microwave oven 10 minutes or until a wooden pick inserted in center comes out clean. Turn dish 4 or 5 times. Serve while warm with Sherry Sauce (directions follow). Makes about 8 servings.

Sherry Sauce. Beat together ¼ cup soft butter or margarine and 1 cup powdered sugar until light and creamy. Beat 2 egg whites until foamy; then beat in 1 tablespoon granulated sugar until whites form stiff, moist peaks. Stir into butter mixture with ¼ cup cream Sherry. Cook, uncovered, in the microwave oven 30 seconds to warm through.

Creamy Pumpkin Custards

Made with canned pumpkin, these tasty custards can be served at any season topped with sweetened whipped cream and your favorite chopped nuts.

2 eggs
¼ teaspoon salt
¼ cup maple syrup
¾ cup canned pumpkin
½ teaspoon ground cinnamon
¼ teaspoon *each* ground nutmeg and ginger
1 can (about 5 oz.) evaporated milk
Sweetened whipped cream
Chopped nuts

Beat eggs slightly; then add salt, syrup, pumpkin, cinnamon, nutmeg, ginger, and milk; beat until blended. Fill 4 custard cups (6 oz. *each*) with equal amounts of pumpkin mixture. Cook, uncovered, in the microwave oven 4 to 4½ minutes or until just set when jiggled; stir each cup 4 times during cooking and reposition cups for more even cooking. Chill. To serve, garnish with sweetened whipped cream and chopped nuts. Makes 4 servings.

Individual Baked Custards

Light, uncomplicated custards make a pleasant finish to any meal. Baked in individual cups, they can be made a day ahead.

1¾ cups milk
3 eggs
¼ cup sugar
⅛ teaspoon salt
½ teaspoon vanilla
Assorted Garnishes (suggestions follow)

In a glass measure, heat milk, uncovered, in the microwave oven 2 minutes. Beat together eggs, sugar, salt, and vanilla. Beating continuously, pour scalded milk into eggs. Pour into 4 custard cups (6 oz. *each*). Cook, uncovered, 4 to 4½ minutes or until just set when jiggled; stir each cup four times during cooking and reposition cups for more even cooking. Chill, uncovered, 1 hour. Then cover and chill if storing longer. Garnish as desired. Makes 4 servings.

Assorted Garnishes. Top each custard with one of the following: dash of ground nutmeg or cinnamon; sprinkling of toasted coconut; sliced sweetened strawberries or raspberries; sliced peaches; banana slices rolled in orange juice and chopped nuts; whipped cream.

Lemon Date Pudding

Lemon peel and juice give a refreshing tang to this moist fruit and nut pudding.

       1 cup water
       1 cup pitted dates, chopped
       1 teaspoon soda
    1¼ cups all-purpose flour (unsifted)
       1 cup chopped walnuts or pecans
    ¼ teaspoon *each* baking powder and salt
    ¼ cup butter or margarine
       1 cup sugar
       1 egg
       1 teaspoon grated lemon peel
       1 tablespoon lemon juice
       2 tablespoons sugar
       1 teaspoon ground cinnamon
         Whipped cream or ice cream

In a small bowl, heat water to boiling in the microwave oven (about 2½ minutes). Add dates and soda to water; set aside.

Combine flour, nuts, baking powder, and salt; set aside. With an electric mixer, beat butter and 1 cup sugar together until fluffy. Beat in egg, lemon peel, and lemon juice. Using low speed, blend in flour mixture, then date mixture. Evenly spoon batter into an 8-inch-square baking dish.

Combine 2 tablespoons sugar and cinnamon; sprinkle over batter. Cook, uncovered, in the microwave oven 10 minutes or until a wooden pick inserted in center comes out clean; turn dish 4 or 5 times. Cool in dish. Serve with whipped cream or ice cream. Makes about 8 servings.

Steamed Apple Dumplings

Dumplings are a "natural" for the microwave—the moist cooking steams them perfectly. Whole wheat biscuit mix shortens preparation time and gives the dumplings an appealing golden hue.

       4 large tart apples, peeled, cored, and sliced
         (5 to 6 cups)
       2 tablespoons water
       1 tablespoon lemon juice
    ½ teaspoon grated lemon peel
    ¾ cup sugar
    ¼ teaspoon ground cinnamon
    ⅛ teaspoon ground nutmeg
         Dumplings (recipe follows)
         Half-and-half (light cream)

Mix apples, water, lemon juice, lemon peel, sugar, cinnamon, and nutmeg in an 8-inch round baking dish. Cover and cook in the microwave oven 6 minutes, stirring gently 3 times. Using a large spoon, drop 6 dumplings on top of fruit, making a circle around edge of dish. Cook, uncovered, 7 minutes or until dumplings are cooked through when slashed; turn dish every 2 minutes. Let stand 5 to 10 minutes. Serve warm with cream to pour over. Makes 6 servings.

Dumplings. In a small bowl, stir together 1 cup whole wheat biscuit mix, ¼ cup firmly packed brown sugar, ½ teaspoon ground cinnamon, ¼ teaspoon ground nutmeg, and 3 tablespoons finely chopped nuts. Combine ⅓ cup milk and ½ teaspoon vanilla; add to dry mixture, stirring just until blended.

Sugar Crumb Coffee Cake

A quick breakfast idea for family or friends, this coffee cake bakes in just 5 minutes to serve hot to early risers or reheated to latecomers.

    1¼ cups all-purpose flour (unsifted)
    1¼ teaspoons baking powder
    ¼ teaspoon salt
    ¼ cup (⅛ lb.) butter or margarine
    ⅔ cup sugar
       1 egg
    ⅓ cup milk
       1 teaspoon vanilla
         Crumb Topping (recipe follows)
         Ground cinnamon

Stir together flour, baking powder, and salt. With an electric mixer, beat butter and sugar thoroughly; then beat in egg. On low speed, blend in flour mixture, milk, and vanilla. Spoon into an 8-inch-square baking dish. Sprinkle with Crumb Topping, then with cinnamon. Cook, uncovered, in the microwave oven 5 minutes or until a wooden pick inserted in center comes out clean; turn dish twice. Cut in 2½-inch squares. Makes 9 servings.

Crumb Topping. In a small bowl, mix together ¼ cup all-purpose flour, 2 tablespoons powdered sugar, and ½ teaspoon ground cinnamon. With 2 knives, cut in 3 tablespoons butter or margarine until mixture is crumbly. Stir in ¼ cup *each* chopped nuts and coconut.

Breakfast Graham Cake

For a spring brunch, serve cake topped with sweetened whipped cream and sugared sliced strawberries.

  3 eggs, separated
  1 cup granulated sugar
  ½ cup (¼ lb.) softened butter or margarine
  ¾ cup milk
  1 teaspoon vanilla
  2 cups graham cracker crumbs (about 32 individual cracker squares)
  ⅛ teaspoon salt
  1 teaspoon baking powder
    Powdered sugar
    Sweetened whipped cream
    Strawberries, sliced and sweetened to taste

Beat egg whites until frothy; then gradually beat in ¼ cup of the granulated sugar until stiff, moist peaks form; set aside.

Beat together butter and remaining ¾ cup granulated sugar until well blended. Beat in egg yolks; then blend in milk and vanilla. Stir together cracker crumbs, salt, and baking powder; blend into egg yolk mixture. Gently fold beaten whites into crumb mixture until blended.

Pour into an 8-inch-square baking dish (first line it with waxed paper if you plan to turn cake out of pan to serve). Cook, uncovered, in the microwave oven, 10 minutes or until a wooden pick inserted in center comes out clean. Turn dish 4 or 5 times. Let cool about 10 minutes; then turn out onto a wire rack, if desired, to cool completely. Dust with powdered sugar before serving. Offer whipped cream and strawberries to spoon over top. Makes 8 servings.

Orange Syrup Yogurt Cake

Orange syrup complements this lemon-flavored yogurt cake. It is quick to make. As with muffins, you have to be careful not to overbeat the batter.

    Orange Syrup (recipe follows)
  1 carton (8 oz.) unflavored yogurt
  ¾ cup sugar
  ¼ cup melted butter or margarine
  2 eggs
  1 teaspoon lemon extract
  1½ cups all-purpose flour (unsifted)
  ¾ teaspoon soda

Prepare Orange Syrup; set aside. In a large bowl, stir together yogurt, sugar, and butter until well blended. With a wooden spoon, beat in eggs, one at a time, until mixture is smooth; stir in lemon extract.

Stir together flour and soda. Add all at once to yogurt mixture and stir just until smooth (about 45 strokes); do not overbeat. Pour batter into an 8-inch-square baking dish. Cook, uncovered, in the microwave oven 8 to 9 minutes or until a wooden pick inserted in center comes out clean; turn dish 2 or 3 times. Allow to stand on flat surface about 5 minutes; then place on cooling rack. With a fork, pierce warm cake deeply all over surface. Pour warm Orange Syrup through a wire strainer over cake; let stand about 30 minutes before serving. Makes 8 servings.

Orange Syrup. Combine ¾ cup *each* sugar and hot water and 1 tablespoon grated orange peel in a glass quart measure. Cook, uncovered, in the microwave oven until boiling rapidly, stirring at least once to dissolve sugar; then boil 3 minutes. Let cool 5 to 10 minutes. Stir in ¼ cup Cointreau or other orange-flavored liqueur.

Apricot Upside-down Gingercake

Fresh apricot halves make an upside-down gingercake attractive to serve and delicious to eat. When fresh ones aren't available, use well-drained canned apricot halves.

  7 tablespoons butter or margarine
  ⅓ cup firmly packed brown sugar
  12 fresh apricots (about 1 lb.), pitted and halved
  ½ cup granulated sugar
  1 egg
  ½ cup light molasses
  ⅓ cup milk
  1½ cups all-purpose flour (unsifted)
  1 teaspoon *each* soda, ground cinnamon, and ground ginger
  ¼ teaspoon salt
    Red candied cherry halves (optional)

In a 10-inch round baking dish, melt 3 tablespoons of the butter in the microwave oven 2 minutes. Distribute brown sugar evenly over butter; then evenly arrange apricot halves, cut sides down, in a single layer over brown sugar.

In a large bowl, beat sugar and remaining butter until creamy. Add egg, molasses, and milk; beat until well blended. Stir together flour, soda, cinnamon, ginger, and salt. Add to creamed mixture, beating until blended. Spread batter over apricot halves. Cook, uncovered, in the microwave oven for 12 to 14 minutes or until top of cake looks dry; turn dish 3 or 4 times. Let stand for 5 minutes. Loosen edge and then invert onto a serving plate. If you wish, place a cherry half in center of each apricot. Serve warm. Makes 6 servings.

Chocolate Applesauce Cake

This moist, spicy cake packs and transports well, making it a good candidate for brown-bag lunches.

½ cup salad oil
2 squares (1 oz. *each*) semisweet baking chocolate
2 cups all-purpose flour (unsifted)
1 cup granulated sugar
1½ tablespoons cornstarch
2 teaspoons soda
1 teaspoon ground cinnamon
½ teaspoon ground nutmeg
¼ teaspoon *each* ground cloves and salt
½ cup raisins
1 cup chopped nuts
1 can (16 oz.) applesauce
Powdered sugar

Combine oil and chocolate in a small glass bowl. Place in the microwave oven and cook, uncovered, 1½ minutes or until chocolate it melted; set aside.
Stir together flour, granulated sugar, corn-

starch, soda, cinnamon, nutmeg, cloves, salt, raisins, and nuts. Add chocolate mixture and applesauce, mixing until well blended. Pour into a 7 by 11-inch baking dish. Cook, uncovered, 12 to 13 minutes or until a wooden pick inserted in center comes out clean; turn dish 3 or 4 times. Let cake cool on a wooden board. Before serving, dust with sifted powdered sugar. Makes 6 to 8 servings.

Caramel Baked Apples

Brown sugar and whipping cream blend into a delicious caramel-flavored sauce when cooked. For extra appeal, spoon some over each serving of baked apple.

4 large, tart apples (such as Pippin, Granny Smith, Rome Beauties)
½ cup firmly packed brown sugar
1 tablespoon *each* raisins and chopped nuts (optional)
Ground cinnamon
⅓ cup whipping cream

Core apples and peel off skin from top half of each apple. Arrange in an 8-inch round baking dish. Partially fill center of each apple with brown sugar; then stuff with nuts and raisins, if desired. Add more brown sugar to fill centers. Spoon any remaining brown sugar into bottom of dish. Sprinkle each apple lightly with ground cinnamon. Then drizzle whipping cream slowly over apples, pouring some into the brown sugar in each core. Cook, uncovered, in the microwave oven 8 to 10 minutes until apples are tender when pierced with fork; turn dish 2 or 3 times. Transfer apples to individual serving dishes. Cook remaining brown sugar and whipping cream without a cover 1½ to 2 minutes or until mixture boils vigorously; stir well. Spoon sauce evenly over each apple; serve warm. Makes 4 servings.

Cinnamon Baked Apple

Core 1 small, tart apple and place it in a small shallow bowl. Fill center with 1 tablespoon tiny red cinnamon candies. Cook, uncovered, in the microwave oven 2 to 3 minutes or until apple is tender when pierced.

Gingery Rhubarb

Rhubarb done in the microwave makes a bright-colored dessert. Use fresh or frozen fruit for this recipe. Top with whipped cream.

    5 cups fresh sliced rhubarb or 1 bag (20 oz.)
        frozen unsweetened rhubarb
    1 cup sugar
    2 tablespoons chopped candied ginger
        Whipped cream

If using frozen rhubarb, place fruit in 2-quart baking dish, cover, and cook in the microwave oven 4 to 5 minutes until thawed.

  In same baking dish, cover and cook fresh or thawed frozen rhubarb 5 to 6 minutes or until tender when pierced, stirring carefully once or twice. Stir in sugar and ginger. Cover and cook 1 minute or until sugar dissolves. Spoon into 6 dessert dishes and chill. Serve garnished with whipped cream. Makes 6 servings.

Cherries Jubilee

A glamorous dessert by anyone's measure, Cherries Jubilee can be flamed in front of guests after the Kirsch liqueur is heated 25 seconds in the microwave oven.

    1 bag (16 oz.) frozen pitted dark sweet
        cherries, unsweetened
    1 tablespoon cornstarch
    ⅓ cup currant jelly
    2 tablespoons sugar
    ¼ cup Kirsch (cherry brandy)
        About 1½ pints vanilla ice cream

To thaw frozen cherries, pierce top of bag with a fork in several places and cook in the microwave oven 3 minutes; let stand 5 to 10 minutes. Drain juices into a 1½ to 2-quart serving dish. Smoothly mix in cornstarch; then add jelly and sugar. Cook, uncovered, 2½ minutes until thickened and clear, stirring 2 or 3 times. Stir in cherries and any additional juice. Cook, covered, 3 minutes until cherries are heated through. Warm Kirsch in a glass measuring cup 25 seconds and then pour it over hot cherry sauce and ignite. Stir until flames subside. Spoon hot cherries over ice cream. Makes 6 servings.

Flaming Bananas Guadalajara

Turn down the lights before you flame the liqueur-coated bananas. They'll perform on their own.

    3 tablespoons butter or magarine
    3 tablespoons firmly packed brown sugar
        Dash ground nutmeg
    ½ teaspoon grated orange peel
    4 firm-ripe bananas, peeled and sliced ½
        inch thick
    2 tablespoons *each* rum and coffee-flavored
        liqueur
        About 1½ pints vanilla or coffee ice cream

In a shallow 1½ to 2-quart serving dish, melt butter in the microwave oven 1 to 2 minutes or until bubbly. Stir in sugar, nutmeg, and orange peel. Cook, uncovered, 2 minutes to dissolve sugar; stir well. Add bananas, stirring lightly to coat with butter mixture. Cover and cook 2 minutes or until bananas begin to soften. Combine rum and liqueur in a glass measuring cup; heat 25 seconds. Pour over bananas and ignite; then spoon flaming sauce over bananas until flames subside. Serve bananas over scoops of ice cream. Makes about 6 servings.

*Use full power setting on all recipes
unless otherwise indicated*

Index